Steck-Vaughn

Language
Exercises
Book 5

Rigby • Saxon • Steck-Vaughn

www.HarcourtAchieve.com
1.800.531.5015

Acknowledgments

Macmillan/McGraw-Hill School Publishing Company: Pronunciation Key, reprinted with permission of the publisher, from *Macmillan School Dictionary 1*. Copyright © 1990 Macmillan Publishing Company, a division of Macmillan, Inc.

LANGUAGE EXERCISES Series:

Book 1	Book 4	Book 7
Book 2	Book 5	Book 8
Book 3	Book 6	Review

ISBN 1-4190-1873-6
ISBN 978-1-4190-1873-2

© 2006 Harcourt Achieve Inc.

7 8 0982 12 11
4500291122

Table of Contents

Unit 6 Study Skills

Final Reviews

A. Write S before each pair of synonyms, A before each pair of antonyms, and H before each pair of homonyms.

_____ **1.** river, stream

_____ **2.** new, knew

_____ **3.** ugly, pretty

_____ **4.** threw, through

B. Write the homograph for the pair of meanings.

_____ **a.** a formal dance   **b.** a round object

C. Write P before each word with a prefix, S before each word with a suffix, and C before each compound word.

_____ **1.** shoelace

_____ **2.** mistrust

_____ **3.** firmness

_____ **4.** downstairs

D. Write the words that make up each contraction.

_____ **1.** won't

_____ **2.** he'll

E. Write D before the declarative sentence, IM before the imperative sentence, E before the exclamatory sentence, and IN before the interrogative sentence. Then circle the simple subject, and underline the simple predicate in each sentence.

_____ **1.** Happy days are here again!

_____ **2.** What do you mean by that?

_____ **3.** I really like my life right now.

_____ **4.** You should take it one day at a time.

F. Write CS before the sentence with a compound subject. Write CP before the sentence with a compound predicate.

_____ **1.** Apples and oranges are my favorite fruits.

_____ **2.** The wind howled and shrieked.

G. Write CS before the compound sentence. Write RO before the run-on sentence.

_____ **1.** Since it was raining we went inside, we sat and watched it rain.

_____ **2.** It didn't stop raining, so we played card games.

H. Underline the common nouns, and circle the proper nouns in the sentence.

José told Rachel that her dog had been found in the park.

I. Write the correct possessive noun to complete the second sentence.

The headlight of our car burned out. Our _____ headlight burned out.

J. Write **A** if the underlined verb is an action verb, **L** if it is a linking verb, or **H** if it is a helping verb.

_____ **1.** We <u>were</u> waiting our turn.

_____ **2.** It <u>felt</u> good to be there.

_____ **3.** We <u>helped</u> as often as possible.

K. Write <u>past</u>, <u>present</u>, or <u>future</u> to show the tense of each underlined verb.

_____ **1.** Someone <u>will come</u> soon.

_____ **2.** They <u>left</u> an hour later.

_____ **3.** She <u>is walking</u> with her children.

L. Circle the correct verb in each sentence.
1. (Do, Did) you (see, saw) what happened?
2. He (drink, drank) the water and then (broke, break) the glass.
3. She has (wrote, written) a hit song and has (sang, sung) it on TV.
4. We (eaten, ate) a big meal and (begun, began) to get sleepy.

M. Write **SP** before the sentence that has a subject pronoun, **OP** before the sentence that has an object pronoun, and **PP** before the sentence that has a possessive pronoun.

_____ **1.** My grandparents were successful farmers.

_____ **2.** They always lived out in the country.

_____ **3.** Mother told me about the farm.

N. On the line before each sentence, write <u>adjective</u> or <u>adverb</u> to describe the underlined word.

_____ **1.** Exercise is part of my <u>daily</u> activities.

_____ **2.** I run <u>often</u>.

O. In the sentence below, underline each prepositional phrase, and circle each preposition.

An oil spot was on the floor of the garage.

P. Circle the correct word in each sentence.

1. (Teach, Learn) me how to bake.
2. We will have a (well, good) time together.
3. Get the eggs, and (sit, set) them on the counter.
4. Now (sit, set) on the stool.
5. You (can, may) separate the eggs.

Q. In the letter below, underline letters that should be capitalized, and add punctuation where needed.

487 e deer run

sacramento ca 94099

feb 27 2006

dear luke

whats it like living in california ___ i cant even imagine it ___ the postcards you sent were fantastic ___ it will be fun to come and visit ___ im worried about earthquakes, though ___

take care of yourself ___

your friend

paul

R. Expand the meaning of the sentence base below.

Students created. _____

S. Write a topic sentence and two sentences with descriptive supporting details on the topic of pollution.

_____

_____

_____

T. Number the following directions in order.

_____ 1. Turn on the dishwasher.

_____ 2. Load dirty dishes in the machine.

_____ 3. Put soap in the dispenser.

U. Use the dictionary entry below to answer the questions.

cobbler (kob′ lər) *n.* **1.** a mender of boots or shoes: *The cobbler was an expert.* **2.** a deep-dish fruit pie: *Cherry cobbler is my favorite dessert.*

n.	noun
pron.	pronoun
v.	verb
adj.	adjective
adv.	adverb
prep.	preposition

1. What part of speech is the word <u>cobbler</u>? _____

2. Would <u>cobweb</u> be before or after <u>cobbler</u>? _____

3. Would <u>coal / code</u> be the guide words for <u>cobbler</u>? _____

V. Write <u>title page</u>, <u>copyright page</u>, <u>table of contents</u>, or <u>index</u> to tell where you would find the information.

_____ 1. the page on which a chapter begins

_____ 2. the author's name

_____ 3. the year a book was published

W. Use the sample encyclopedia entry to answer the questions.

PARROT A parrot is any of a number of tropical birds. It has a short, hooked beak and brightly colored feathers. Some species can imitate human speech. *See also* PARAKEET.

1. What is this article about? _____

2. What is the cross-reference? _____

_____

Below is a list of the sections on *Check What You Know* and the pages on which the skills in each section are taught. If you missed any questions, turn to the pages listed, and practice the skills. Then correct the problems you missed on *Check What You Know*.

Section	Practice Page	Section	Practice Page	Section	Practice Page
Unit 1		*Unit 3*		*Unit 4*	
A	5–7	H	31, 32	Q	60–64, 66
B	8	I	34, 35	*Unit 5*	
C	9, 11	J	36, 37, 41	R	73
D	10	K	38, 39	S	74–77, 80, 81
		L	40, 42–45	*Unit 6*	
Unit 2		M	46, 47	T	87
E	16–18, 20, 21	N	48–52	U	88–92
F	23, 24	O	53	V	93
G	25, 26	P	54, 55	W	94

Synonyms

> ■ A **synonym** is a word that has the same or nearly the same meaning as one or more other words.
>   EXAMPLES: help - aid - assist, cold - chilly - wintry

A. Write one synonym for each word below. Write another synonym in a short phrase. Underline the synonym in the phrase.

1. small   _____little_____   _____<u>tiny</u> bug_____

2. enormous   _____   _____

3. vehicle   _____   _____

4. select   _____   _____

5. complete   _____   _____

6. river   _____   _____

7. permit   _____   _____

8. speedy   _____   _____

B. For each word in parentheses, write a synonym in the blank.

1. Many trees in an old forest are (high) _____ .

2. Underneath them grow (lower) _____ trees and plants.

3. As the (aged) _____ trees die, they make room for others.

4. Sometimes fires will (destroy) _____ the entire forest.

5. Then from the (charred) _____ earth sprout new plants.

6. They all begin their (stretch) _____ for the sky again.

C. Write three sentences about the forest. In each sentence, use a synonym for one of the words below. Underline the synonym.

begin	lofty	soil

1. _____

2. _____

3. _____

Antonyms

> ■ An **antonym** is a word that has the opposite meaning of another word.   EXAMPLES: hot - cold, tall - short

A. Write an antonym for the underlined word in each phrase below.

1. <u>dark</u> blue _____

2. <u>busy</u> worker _____

3. <u>up</u> the hill _____

4. <u>noisy</u> play _____

5. <u>north</u> wind _____

6. <u>buy</u> a car _____

7. time of <u>day</u> _____

8. <u>bitter</u> taste _____

9. <u>come</u> now _____

10. <u>good</u> dog _____

11. <u>small</u> bird _____

12. <u>rough</u> road _____

13. <u>black</u> coat _____

14. <u>above</u> the neck _____

15. <u>frowning</u> face _____

16. <u>under</u> the bridge _____

17. <u>pretty</u> color _____

18. <u>cold</u> water _____

19. feeling <u>strong</u> _____

20. <u>wide</u> belt _____

21. <u>unhappy</u> face _____

22. <u>east</u> side _____

23. <u>cool</u> breeze _____

24. <u>stop</u> the car _____

25. <u>heavy</u> jacket _____

26. <u>long</u> story _____

27. <u>give</u> a gift _____

28. <u>difficult</u> task _____

B. For each word in parentheses, write an antonym in the blank.

We were very (sad) _____ to be on vacation. It

was the (last) _____ time we had been able to (stay)

_____ in a long time, and this one would be really (boring)

_____ . We rented a cabin in the (low) _____

mountains of Colorado. We were hoping for (hot) _____

and snowy weather so we could ski. The (last) _____ thing

we did when we got to the cabin was (pack) _____ our

clothes. Then we hiked around (inside) _____ . We liked

being in such a (terrible) _____ place.

Homonyms

- **Homonyms** are words that are pronounced alike but are spelled differently and have different meanings.
   EXAMPLES: I'll – aisle   two – too – to

A. Write a short phrase that includes a homonym for each word below. Circle each homonym.

1. haul _____long (hall)_____

2. road _____

3. sum _____

4. way _____

5. new _____

6. meat _____

- **Two** is a number. **Too** means "also," "besides," or "more than enough." **To** means "toward." It is also used with such words as <u>be</u>, <u>sing</u>, <u>play</u>, and other action words.

B. Fill in the blanks with <u>two</u>, <u>too</u>, or <u>to</u>.

1. Ben was _____ frightened _____ utter a word.

2. He had heard the strange sound _____ times.

3. He went _____ his room upstairs, _____ steps at a time.

   But he heard it there, _____.

4. He decided _____ call his friend who lived _____ blocks away.

   It seemed the only thing _____ do!

- **Their** means "belonging to them." **There** means "in that place." **They're** is a contraction of the words <u>they</u> <u>are</u>.

C. Underline the correct word in parentheses.

1. They are over (their, there, they're) standing in (their, there, they're) yard.

2. (Their, There, They're) waiting to go visit (their, there, they're) friends.

3. (Their, There, They're) going to leave for (their, there, they're) vacation.

Lesson 4 — Homographs

> ■ **Homographs** are words that are spelled the same but have different meanings. They may also be pronounced differently.
> EXAMPLE: <u>desert</u> meaning "a barren, dry place" and <u>desert</u> also meaning "to abandon"

A. Read each sentence and the two meanings for the underlined word. Circle the meaning that tells how the word is used in the sentence.

1. The soldiers' <u>arms</u> were old and rusty.
   a. parts of the body   b. weapons for war

2. Several had made <u>bats</u> from fallen tree limbs.
   a. flying mammals   b. rounded wooden clubs

3. The <u>long</u> war had made them all tired.
   a. extending over a considerable time   b. to wish for

4. They were all ready to go <u>back</u> home.
   a. part of the body   b. to a place from which a person came

5. They hoped someone would <u>lead</u> them to safety.
   a. soft, gray metal   b. to show the way

B. Write the homograph for each pair of meanings below. The first letter of each word is given for you.

1. a. sound made with fingers   b. a metal fastener   s_____

2. a. lame walk or step   b. not stiff   l_____

3. a. use oars to move a boat   b. a noisy fight   r_____

4. a. a tree covering   b. the sound a dog makes   b_____

5. a. to press flat   b. a yellow vegetable   s_____

C. Write pairs of sentences that show two different meanings for each homograph below. Use a dictionary if necessary.

1. school _____

_____

2. pupil _____

_____

- A **prefix** or a **suffix** added to a base word changes the meaning of the word.
  EXAMPLE: <u>re-</u> meaning "again" + the base word <u>do</u> = <u>redo</u> meaning "to do again"
- <u>Re-</u> means "again," <u>pre-</u> means "before," <u>mis-</u> means "wrongly" or "not," <u>-able</u> means "that can be," <u>-less</u> means "without," <u>-ness</u> means "state of being."

A. Write the word formed by each combination. Then write the definition of the new word.

1. kind + ness = _____

2. pre + date = _____

3. help + less = _____

4. re + made = _____

B. Read each sentence. Use one of the prefixes or suffixes and the base word below each blank to form a new word. Write the new word in the blank.

mis-   -ful   pre-   -less   re-   -ness

1. Terry _____ her vacation by viewing the photographs
   (lives)

   she took.

2. She spends _____ hours enjoying the mountain scenery.
   (end)

3. Her favorite shot shows a mountain sunset just before

   _____ settled over their campsite.
   (dark)

4. John didn't see Terry's look of fright when a bear made

   a _____ raid on the garbage can.
   (dawn)

5. John had _____ the camera directions in the dim light.
   (read)

6. He did, however, get a shot of the bear's _____ cubs.
   (delight)

> ■ A **contraction** is a word formed by joining two other words.
> An apostrophe shows where a letter or letters have been
> left out.   EXAMPLES: it is = it's   we will = we'll

A. Write the contraction formed by the words.

1. who + is = _____

2. could + not = _____

3. they + have = _____

4. I + will = _____

5. does + not = _____

6. should + have = _____

7. you + would = _____

8. I + have = _____

9. that + is = _____

10. did + not = _____

11. let + us = _____

12. they + are = _____

**B. Use the contractions below to complete each sentence.
Write the contractions on the lines.**

| can't | couldn't | he'll | I'm | it's | I've | Let's |
| She's | wasn't | What'll | What's | Where's | | |

1. It _____ quite show time.

2. José called out, "_____ Pearl?"

3. "What?" shouted Sara. "_____ not here yet?"

4. "No, and _____ looked everywhere."

5. "The show _____ go on without the star," Sara wailed.

6. Sara added, "_____ we do?"

7. "_____ ask Adam," José suggested.

8. "Yes," said Sara, "_____ know what to do."

9. Just then a voice called, "_____ all the excitement?"

10. "Pearl, _____ you!" Sara and José exclaimed.

11. "Yes," said Pearl, "I know _____ late."

12. Pearl added, "I _____ find my costume!"

Lesson 7

Compound Words

> ■ **Compound words** may be two words written as one, two words joined by a hyphen, or two separate words.
> EXAMPLES: sunlight   ho-hum   easy chair

A. Draw a line between the two words that form each compound word below.

1. highway	6. fire drill	11. highrise
2. old-time	7. barefoot	12. earthquake
3. full moon	8. baby-sitter	13. half-mast
4. snowflake	9. splashdown	14. bulldog
5. air conditioner	10. sweatshirt	15. skateboard

B. Use two of the words below to form a compound word that will complete each numbered sentence. Write the word on the blank.

after	back	come	hard	hood	neighbor	noon	out	ware	yard

1. Jan and I bought a hammer and nails at a _____ store.

2. Part of the fence in our _____ was broken.

3. It took most of the _____ to repair the fence.

4. We were proud of the _____.

5. Our fence was the finest in the _____.

C. Use the second word part of each compound word to make the next compound word. Write the new word.

1. clubhouse — a building used by a club

   _____houseboat_____ — a boat that people can live in

   _____boathouse_____ — a house for storing boats

2. teacup — a cup for drinking tea

   _____ — a cake the size of a cup

   _____ — a circular walking game in which players may win a cake

Review

A. Write **S** before each pair of synonyms. Write **A** before each pair of antonyms. Write **H** before each pair of homonyms.

1. _____ more, less
2. _____ rich, wealthy
3. _____ laugh, cry
4. _____ cent, scent
5. _____ neat, tidy

6. _____ save, spend
7. _____ late, tardy
8. _____ sew, so
9. _____ heel, heal
10. _____ join, connect

11. _____ steel, steal
12. _____ certain, sure
13. _____ wait, weight
14. _____ false, untrue
15. _____ refuse, accept

B. Write the correct homograph for the pair of lines in each sentence.

1. I found my red ink _____ in the dog's _____ .

2. Dropping the tennis _____ on the glass table made quite a _____ .

3. I couldn't _____ watching the _____ cub search for its mother.

4. It took a short time to _____ the building when it became _____ there was a fire.

5. When he said that to you, he didn't _____ to be _____ .

C. Add one of the following prefixes or suffixes to each underlined word to fit the meaning. Write the new word that is formed.

re-	pre-	mis-	-ness	-able	-less

1. to <u>wire</u> again _____
2. without <u>hope</u> _____
3. to <u>soak</u> before _____
4. able to be <u>washed</u> _____
5. wrongly <u>shapen</u> _____
6. state of being <u>good</u> _____

7. without <u>humor</u> _____
8. to <u>do</u> again _____
9. able to be <u>removed</u> _____
10. to <u>view</u> before _____
11. state of being <u>strange</u> _____
12. wrongly <u>spelled</u> _____

D. Write the words that mean the same thing as the underlined contraction.

1. <u>What's</u> the reason the Franklins are moving? _____

2. <u>They've</u> decided the schools are better in Aston. _____

3. I guess <u>you'll</u> get to go see their new house. _____

4. They told me <u>I'd</u> have to come visit soon. _____

5. Do the children think <u>they'll</u> like the new school? _____

E. Combine the words below to form six compound words. Write a sentence for each word on the lines.

back	night	loud	shore	tool	news
yard	sea	paper	time	speaker	box

1. _____

2. _____

3. _____

4. _____

5. _____

6. _____

F. In the paragraph below, underline the contractions, and circle the compound words. Then write each marked word and the two words from which it is made on the lines.

> I received a postcard from my friends. They will be traveling overseas in Europe throughout the summer. I believe that they're overdoing it. Why try to see everything in one trip?

1. _____   _____

2. _____   _____

3. _____   _____

4. _____   _____

5. _____   _____

6. _____   _____

A. Read each phrase and the list of words beneath it. Write S before each word that is a synonym of the first word in the phrase. Write A before each word that is an antonym.

1. break a window

_____ repair

_____ shatter

_____ mend

_____ smash

2. clean air

_____ pure

_____ polluted

_____ impure

_____ fresh

3. strong legs

_____ powerful

_____ sturdy

_____ weak

_____ athletic

B. Choose a synonym or antonym from each of the three groups above. Write a sentence using each word.

1. _____

2. _____

3. _____

C. Use each pair of homonyms below in a sentence.

1. hall, haul _We had to haul the piano down the hall to the music room._

2. ad, add _____

3. chilly, chili _____

4. band, banned _____

5. allowed, aloud _____

D. Write about a forest fire. Use as many of the pairs of homographs below as you can. The pairs need not be in the same sentence.

blaze, blaze   bear, bear   bark, bark   wind, wind

_____

_____

_____

_____

_____

E. Add a prefix or a suffix to each numbered word. Form a new word that means the same as the definition given. Use the new word in a sentence.

| -less | -ness | re- | pre- | -able | mis- |

1. use, "of no use" That broken shoelace is useless to me.

2. shy, "state of being shy" _____

3. pay, "to pay before" _____

4. write, "to write again" _____

5. count, "to count wrongly" _____

6. read, "able to be read" _____

F. Below each sentence are three words. Circle the two words that can form a compound word to complete the sentence. Write the compound word.

1. The roof of the house looked silver in the _____.
   light   car   moon

2. Did you suffer _____ on your skiing trip?
   frost   crystal   bite

3. The _____ is an amazing part of the body.
   sight   ball   eye

4. The moon was at its highest point at _____.
   night   summer   mid

5. Were you able to _____ the cause of the problem?
   pin   point   ball

G. Write all the contractions you know that include each word below. Then use one of the contractions you formed in a sentence about a game you like to play.

1. will _____

   Sentence: _____

2. is _____

   Sentence: _____

3. I _____

   Sentence: _____

Recognizing Sentences

> ■ A **sentence** is a group of words that expresses a complete thought.   EXAMPLE: Many readers like stories about dogs.

A. Some of the groups of words below are sentences, and some are not. Write <u>S</u> before each group that is a sentence.

_____ 1. One famous dog story.

_____ 2. First appeared in a well-known magazine.

_____ 3. You may have read this famous story.

_____ 4. A collie named Lassie, who was owned by a poor farmer in Yorkshire, England.

_____ 5. To make money for his family.

_____ 6. The farmer sold Lassie to a wealthy duke.

_____ 7. Lassie was loyal to her first master, however.

_____ 8. Taken hundreds of miles from Yorkshire.

_____ 9. She found her way back to her first home.

_____ 10. The story became a book and then a movie.

_____ 11. Helped two child actors on their way to stardom.

_____ 12. The real-life Lassie was a dog named Toots.

_____ 13. Toots was the companion of Eric Knight, the author of the story.

_____ 14. Lived in Yorkshire as a boy, but in the United States as an adult.

_____ 15. Knight died before his story, "Lassie Come Home," became famous.

_____ 16. Was killed in World War II.

_____ 17. Toots died on Knight's farm two years later.

B. Write a sentence about one of your favorite books.

_____

■ A **declarative** sentence makes a statement.
  EXAMPLE: The telephone is ringing.
■ An **interrogative** sentence asks a question.
  EXAMPLE: Where are you going?

A. Write <u>declarative</u> or <u>interrogative</u> after each sentence in the conversation below.

1. When did you get those new rollerblades? _____

2. I bought them yesterday. _____

3. Don't you think rollerblading is dangerous? _____

4. It's not any more dangerous than skateboarding. _____

5. I would like to learn to rollerblade. _____

6. Will you teach me? _____

7. Do you have a pair of rollerblades? _____

8. No, but I will buy some tomorrow. _____

B. Pretend that you are talking to the inventor of a new way to travel over land, sea, or in the air. Write four questions you'd ask and the inventor's answers. Label each sentence <u>D</u> for declarative or <u>I</u> for interrogative.

1. _____ _____

2. _____ _____

3. _____ _____

4. _____ _____

5. _____ _____

6. _____ _____

7. _____ _____

8. _____ _____

> - An **imperative** sentence expresses a command or a request.
>   EXAMPLES: Answer the telephone. Please don't shout.
> - An **exclamatory** sentence expresses strong or sudden feeling.
>   EXAMPLES: What a great movie! They're off!

A. Write <u>imperative</u> or <u>exclamatory</u> after each sentence.

1. Listen to that strange noise. _____

2. What a weird sound that is! _____

3. Go see what's there. _____

4. Go yourself. _____

5. I'm too scared! _____

6. Then look out the window. _____

7. What a cute kitten that is! _____

8. We shouldn't be scared! _____

9. Go get the kitten. _____

10. Come with me. _____

11. Oh, look! _____

12. Count the rest of the kittens in the basket. _____

13. Read the note attached to the handle. _____

14. What a surprise! _____

B. Write about a time you or someone you know was frightened by something. Use at least one exclamatory sentence and one imperative sentence.

_____

_____

_____

_____

_____

Complete Subjects and Predicates

> - Every sentence has two main parts—a **complete subject** and a **complete predicate.**
> - The complete subject includes all the words that name the person, place, or thing about which something is said.
>   - EXAMPLE: **My sister Sara** plays tennis.
> - The complete predicate includes all the words that tell what the subject is or does.
>   - EXAMPLE: My sister Sara **plays tennis.**

A. Write S before each group of words that may be used as a complete subject. Write P before each group of words that may be used as a complete predicate.

_____ 1. the mayor of our town

_____ 2. has a large town square

_____ 3. celebrate the holidays with parades

_____ 4. an election every four years

_____ 5. a map with every street in town

_____ 6. were planning to build a new swimming pool

B. Complete each sentence by writing a subject or a predicate.

1. All our town council members _____.

2. _____ met in an important meeting.

3. _____ explained the problem.

4. Every interested citizen _____.

5. Our town's first settlers _____.

6. _____ planted crops.

7. _____ has been abandoned for years.

8. _____ should be preserved.

9. Some people _____.

10. _____ will have to come to vote.

11. My entire family _____.

- The **simple subject** of a sentence is the main word in the complete subject.   EXAMPLE: My friends go mushroom hunting. The words My friends make up the complete subject. The word friends is the simple subject.
- If the subject is made up of just one word, that word is both the complete subject and the simple subject.
     EXAMPLE: I go mushroom hunting with my friends.

A. In each sentence below, draw a line between the subject and the predicate. Underline the complete subject. Circle the simple subject.

1. Freshly-picked (morels) are delicious.

2. These mushrooms can be found only in the spring.

3. A rich soil is best for morels.

4. Grassy spots are good places to look.

5. The spring must not be dry or too cold.

6. Damp earth is a good sign that morels may be found.

7. A clear, sunny sky means good hunting.

8. We never know where we'll find morels.

9. Tall, wet grasses often hide them.

10. We must work fast.

11. These spongy little mushrooms do not last long.

12. You might like to join us sometime.

B. Write five sentences about an activity you enjoy. Draw a line between the subject and the predicate. Underline the complete subject. Circle the simple subject.

1. _____

2. _____

3. _____

4. _____

5. _____

Simple Predicates

> - The **simple predicate** of a sentence is a verb within the complete predicate. The verb is an action or being word.
>   EXAMPLE: The Netherlands <u>attracts many tourists</u>. The words <u>attracts many tourists</u> make up the complete predicate. The verb <u>attracts</u> is the simple predicate.
> - The simple predicate may be a one-word verb or a verb of more than one word.
>   EXAMPLES: Joan **likes** tulips. She **is planning** a garden.

A. In each sentence below, draw a line between the subject and the predicate. Underline the complete predicate twice. Circle the simple predicate.

1. Many tourists visit the Netherlands in April or May.
2. The beautiful tulip blooms reach their height of glory during these months.
3. Visitors can see flowers for miles and miles.
4. Joan is dreaming of a trip to the Netherlands someday.
5. She has seen colorful pictures of tulips in catalogs.
6. The catalogs show tulips of all colors in full bloom.
7. Joan is anxious to see the tulips herself.
8. Passing travelers can buy large bunches of flowers.
9. Every Dutch city has flowers everywhere.
10. Flower vases can be found in the cars of some Dutch people.

B. Add a predicate for each subject below. Circle the simple predicate.

1. My neighbor's garden _____.

2. I _____.

3. All of the flowers _____.

C. Write four sentences about a city or a country that you would like to visit or have visited. Draw a line between the subject and the predicate. Underline the complete predicate twice. Circle the simple predicate.

1. _____

2. _____

3. _____

4. _____

> ▪ The subject of an imperative sentence is always the person to whom the command or request is given **(You).** The subject does not appear in the sentence. Therefore, it is called an **understood subject.** EXAMPLES: **(You)** Keep off the grass. **(You)** Close the door, please.

A. On the line after each imperative sentence below, write the understood subject and the simple predicate.

1. Turn left at the next light. _____(You) Turn_____

2. Now turn right on Elm Street. _____

3. Park in front of the house. _____

4. Don't block the driveway. _____

5. Leave enough room for them to leave. _____

6. Help me with the food, please. _____

7. Hold the door open until I get out. _____

8. Get the bag off the back seat. _____

9. Lock the car door, please. _____

10. Check to see that the lights are off. _____

11. Knock harder on the door. _____

12. Try ringing the doorbell. _____

B. Write four imperative sentences about a game or other activity. After each sentence, write the understood subject.

1. _____

2. _____

3. _____

4. _____

■ Two sentences that have different subjects but the same predicate can be combined to make one sentence. The two subjects are joined by <u>and</u>. The subject of the new sentence is called a **compound subject.** EXAMPLE: **Craig** likes tall tales. **Jack** likes tall tales. **Craig and Jack** like tall tales.

A. In each sentence below, underline the subject. If the subject is compound, write <u>C</u> before the sentence.

_____ 1. Paul Bunyan and Babe were the subject of many tall tales.

_____ 2. Babe was Paul's blue ox.

_____ 3. Maine and Minnesota are two of the states that have tall tales about Paul and Babe.

_____ 4. Babe could haul the timber from 640 acres at one time.

_____ 5. Lumberjacks and storytellers liked to tell tall tales about Paul and Babe's great deeds.

B. Combine each pair of sentences below to make a sentence that has a compound subject. Underline the compound subject.

1. Tennessee claims Davy Crockett as its hero. Texas claims Davy Crockett as its hero.

_____

2. Great bravery made Davy Crockett famous. Unusual skills made Davy Crockett famous.

_____

3. True stories about Davy Crockett were passed down. Tall tales about Davy Crockett were passed down.

_____

4. These true stories made Davy Crockett a legend. These tall tales made Davy Crockett a legend.

_____

C. Write a sentence using <u>Paul Bunyan and Davy Crockett</u> as the subject.

_____

_____

> ■ Two sentences that have the same subject but different
> predicates can be combined to make one sentence. The two
> predicates may be joined by <u>or</u>, <u>and</u>, or <u>but</u>. The predicate
> of the sentence is called a **compound predicate.**
>> EXAMPLE: A newspaper **informs its readers.** A newspaper
>> **entertains its readers.** A newspaper **informs and entertains
>> its readers.**

**A. In each sentence below, underline the predicate. If the predicate is
compound, write <u>C</u> before the sentence.**

_____ 1. Our class wrote and printed its own newspaper.

_____ 2. Leslie was named editor-in-chief.

_____ 3. She assigned the stories and approved the final copies.

_____ 4. Wong and several other students were reporters.

_____ 5. They either wrote the news stories or edited the stories.

_____ 6. Wong interviewed a new student and wrote up the interview.

**B. Combine each pair of sentences below to make a sentence that has a
compound predicate. Underline the compound predicate.**

1. Jenny covered the baseball game. Jenny described the best plays.

_____

2. Sue and Kim wrote jokes. Sue and Kim made up puzzles.

_____

3. Luis corrected the news stories. Luis wrote headlines.

_____

4. Alex typed the newspaper. Alex couldn't print the newspaper.

_____

**C. Imagine that you are Luis or Jenny. Write a sentence that has a
compound predicate which could begin the story on the baseball game.**

_____

_____

Simple and Compound Sentences

> ■ A **simple sentence** has one subject and one predicate.
>   EXAMPLE: The United States' presidents / led interesting lives.
> ■ A **compound sentence** is made up of two simple sentences joined by connecting words such as <u>and</u>, <u>but</u>, and <u>or</u>. A comma is placed before the connecting word.
>   EXAMPLE: <u>George Washington</u> <u>led the army in the Revolutionary War</u>, **and** <u>Ulysses S. Grant</u> <u>led it in the Civil War</u>.

A. Draw a line between each subject and predicate. Write <u>S</u> before each simple sentence. Write <u>C</u> before each compound sentence.

_____ 1. George Washington witnessed the first successful balloon flight.

_____ 2. John Adams was our second president, and his son was our sixth.

_____ 3. Thomas Jefferson was very interested in experiments with balloons and submarines.

_____ 4. The British burned the White House in 1814, but President Madison escaped unharmed.

B. Combine each pair of simple sentences below into a compound sentence.

1. Andrew Jackson was called "Old Hickory."
   Zachary Taylor's nickname was "Old Rough and Ready."

   _____

   _____

2. Four presidents had no children. John Tyler had fourteen children.

   _____

   _____

3. Chester A. Arthur put the first bathroom in the White House. Benjamin Harrison put in electric lights.

   _____

   _____

4. Woodrow Wilson coached college football. Ronald Reagan announced baseball games on radio.

   _____

   _____

Correcting Run-on Sentences

> - Two or more sentences that are run together without the correct punctuation are called a **run-on sentence.**
>   EXAMPLE: Animals that carry their young in the mother's pouch are called marsupials, they live mainly in Australia.
> - Correct a run-on sentence by making separate sentences from its parts.
>   EXAMPLE: Animals that carry their young in the mother's pouch are called marsupials. They live mainly in Australia.

A. Separate the run-on sentences below. Write the last word of the first sentence. Place a period after the word. Then write the first word of the second sentence. Be sure to capitalize the word. One run-on sentence is made of three sentences.

1. There are over two hundred kinds of marsupials all live in North or South America or in Australia.

   1. _____ marsupials.
      _____ All _____

2. The kangaroo is the largest marsupial, the male red kangaroo may be up to seven feet tall.

   2. _____
      _____

3. Wallabies are similar to kangaroos, they are smaller than kangaroos, some are the size of a rabbit.

   3. _____
      _____
      _____
      _____

4. Kangaroos and wallabies live only in Australia, their hind feet are larger than their front feet.

   4. _____
      _____

B. Correct the run-on sentences in the paragraph below. Use the proofreader's symbols as shown in parentheses. (The opossum is active at night, it plays dead if frightened.) There will be seven sentences.

Opossums are the only marsupials that live north of
Mexico, they also live in Central and South America.
Opossums are grayish white, they have a long snout,
hairless ears, and a long, hairless tail. Opossums
have fifty teeth, the opossum mother has from five to
twenty babies, each baby is the size of a kidney bean.

A. Label each sentence as follows: Write <u>D</u> in front of each declarative sentence. Write <u>IN</u> in front of each interrogative sentence. Write <u>IM</u> in front of each imperative sentence. Write <u>E</u> in front of each exclamatory sentence. Write <u>X</u> if the group of words is not a sentence.

_____ 1. Did you know that the first bicycle had no pedals?

_____ 2. Very tiring and could not be steered.

_____ 3. The rider pushed himself forward by walking.

_____ 4. Made the first bicycle with pedals in Scotland.

_____ 5. What a great improvement it was!

_____ 6. What did the public think of this bicycle?

_____ 7. Get that machine off the road.

_____ 8. Say today about bicycles?

_____ 9. They're one of the best inventions ever.

_____ 10. Tell me what you think.

_____ 11. I love riding mine!

_____ 12. Maybe we can ride together sometime.

B. In each sentence below, draw a line between the complete subject and the complete predicate. Underline the simple subject once. Underline the simple predicate twice. One sentence has an understood subject. Write the understood subject on the line after that sentence.

1. The next bicycle was known as the "boneshaker." _____

2. Its wheels were made of wood. _____

3. A new feature was iron tires. _____

4. Guess how this bicycle got its name. _____

5. Wire-spoked wheels came next. _____

6. The front wheel gradually increased in size. _____

7. The rear wheel became smaller. _____

8. They began using iron instead of wood for parts. _____

9. An air-filled rubber tire brought comfort. _____

10. More people turned to bicycling for enjoyment. _____

C. Label the sentences below as follows: **SS** if the sentence has a simple subject; **SP** if the sentence has a simple predicate; **CS** if the sentence has a compound subject; and **CP** if the sentence has a compound predicate.

_____ _____ 1. Water is necessary to all life on Earth.

_____ _____ 2. Plants and animals need water to live.

_____ _____ 3. Living things would weaken and die without it.

_____ _____ 4. Some plants and animals eat and breathe underwater.

_____ _____ 5. Other animals live on land and play in water.

D. **Underline each compound subject once and each compound predicate twice. Circle each simple subject and simple predicate.**

1. Rain and sleet are two forms that water can take.

2. Water also becomes snow and hail.

3. Wind tosses and swirls snowflakes into drifts.

4. Sunshine heats and evaporates water.

E. **Write simple or compound before each sentence.**

_____ 1. It was time to leave.

_____ 2. We were taking a trip, so we got up early.

_____ 3. The sun was not up yet, and there was a chill in the air.

_____ 4. We got into the car, and I turned on the heat.

_____ 5. The sunrise was quite beautiful, and we were glad we saw it.

F. **Rewrite the paragraph. Combine simple sentences into compound sentences, and separate run-on sentences.**

It was hot in the car, we put the windows down. The air was fresh. It felt cool on our faces. Larry began to sing he sang off-key. The song was funny. The song was one we all knew. Soon we were all singing, we sounded terrible, we had fun anyway.

_____

_____

_____

_____

A. Two of the groups of words below are sentences, and three are not. Write S before each sentence. Add whatever is needed to the groups of words to make them complete sentences.

_____ 1. The minute Scott heard his name called. _____

_____ 2. Amy was sure that her name would be called next. _____

_____ 3. The feeling of nervousness was mounting. _____

_____ 4. Only three possible names. _____

_____ 5. Amy could hardly. _____

B. Complete each sentence below to make the kind of sentence named.

Declarative   1. An expert is one who _____

Interrogative 2. Why did the expert _____

Imperative   3. Read the _____

Exclamatory   4. What a perfect _____

C. Add to each subject or predicate below whatever is needed to make a sentence. Underline the simple subject once and the simple predicate twice.

1. The dangerous tornado _____.

2. A raging wind storm _____.

3. _____ had flooded the downtown area.

4. Homeowners for several blocks _____.

5. _____ created puddles two feet deep.

6. _____ rescued a helpless motorist.

D. Write three sentences in which You is the understood subject. Include one of the verbs below in each sentence.

hide	do	think	give	walk	sit

1. _____

2. _____

3. _____

E. Write a compound subject for each predicate. Underline the simple predicate twice.

1. _____ opened the special event.

2. _____ were given to the school.

3. _____ presented the awards.

4. _____ received a lot of praise.

F. Write a compound predicate for each subject. Underline the simple subject.

1. The bank robber _____.

2. The undercover detective _____.

3. One innocent bystander _____.

4. The trembling bank clerk _____.

G. Rewrite the sentences below by making one of these improvements: (a) combine sentences by using compound subjects or compound predicates; (b) combine simple sentences to make compound sentences; (c) correct run-on sentences.

1. Alex and Steve were writing a play, they wrote together often.

_____

2. This time they couldn't agree. They argued for hours.

_____

3. Alex would say one thing. Steve would say the opposite.

_____

4. They were both right. They were both wrong. Neither would give in.

_____

5. Finally, Alex stood up, he said he was leaving.

_____

6. Steve couldn't believe it. He couldn't believe that their argument had caused such a serious problem.

_____

7. They glared at each other, they started laughing.

_____

8. They decided to forget the problem. They decided to work together as a team.

_____

Lesson 19 — Nouns

> ■ A **noun** is a word that names a person, place, thing, or quality.   EXAMPLES: Rachel, Chad, city, Montana, shell, animal, love, freedom, happiness

A. Write nouns that name the following:

1. Four people you admire

   _____   _____
   _____   _____

2. Four places you would like to visit

   _____   _____
   _____   _____

3. Six things you use every day

   _____   _____
   _____   _____
   _____   _____

4. Four qualities you would like to have

   _____   _____
   _____   _____

5. Four states in the United States

   _____   _____
   _____   _____

B. Find and underline twenty-six nouns in the sentences below.

1. Every section of the United States has scenes of natural beauty.
2. The tall trees in California are called the giants of the forest.
3. Every fall, tourists go to see the colorful trees in Vermont.
4. Southern coastal cities are proud of their sandy beaches.
5. Colorful flowers and grasses cover the prairies of Texas.
6. Montana and Wyoming boast of majestic mountains.
7. The citizens of every state take pride in the charm of their own state.

> ■ There are two main classes of nouns: **common** and **proper nouns.**
> ■ A **common noun** is a word that names any one of a class of objects.   EXAMPLES: girl, city, dog
> ■ A **proper noun** is the name of a particular person, place, or thing. It begins with a capital letter.
>   EXAMPLES: Sue, Nashville, Digger

A. Write a proper noun for each common noun below.

1. city _____

2. school _____

3. friend _____

4. ocean _____

5. state _____

6. car _____

7. singer _____

8. day _____

9. lake _____

10. street _____

11. game _____

12. river _____

13. woman _____

14. country _____

15. man _____

16. president _____

17. month _____

18. planet _____

B. Write a common noun for each proper noun below.

1. Alaska _____

2. November _____

3. Thanksgiving _____

4. Beth _____

5. December _____

6. Hawaii _____

7. *Call of the Wild* _____

8. Saturday _____

9. Manitoba _____

10. South America _____

11. Dr. Cooke _____

12. Rocky Mountains _____

13. Abraham Lincoln _____

14. Sahara _____

15. Denver _____

16. Mexico _____

17. Saturn _____

18. Jason _____

> ■ A **singular noun** is a noun that names one person, place, or thing.   EXAMPLES: knife, church, boy, mouse
> ■ A **plural noun** is a noun that names more than one person, place, or thing.   EXAMPLES: knives, churches, boys, mice

A. Write S before each singular noun below. Then write its plural form. Write P before each plural noun. Then write its singular form. You may wish to check the spellings in a dictionary.

_____ 1. boots _____

_____ 2. army _____

_____ 3. match _____

_____ 4. maps _____

_____ 5. inches _____

_____ 6. foot _____

_____ 7. hero _____

_____ 8. alley _____

_____ 9. baby _____

_____ 10. women _____

_____ 11. halves _____

_____ 12. skies _____

_____ 13. wife _____

_____ 14. boxes _____

_____ 15. beach _____

_____ 16. book _____

B. Write the plural form of each word below to complete the sentences.

watch	shelf	child	story	monkey	player

1. There are many interesting _____ in that magazine.

2. The cover story on timepieces describes the making of _____.

3. A sports story contains conversations with three of the nation's leading football _____.

4. A do-it-yourself article shows how to build _____ that will hold an aquarium.

5. Unusual _____ and apes are shown in a picture story.

6. This month's special article is a selection of poems and stories by German _____.

- A **possessive noun** shows possession of the noun that follows.   EXAMPLES: mother's car, the dog's bone
- To form the possessive of most singular nouns, add an apostrophe (') and -s.   EXAMPLES: Sally's room, the city's mayor

A. Write the possessive form of the noun in parentheses to complete each phrase.

1. the _____ leash   (dog)

2. the _____ lawn   (neighbor)

3. one of the _____ engines   (plane)

4. _____ greatest ambition   (Ann)

5. to _____ house   (grandmother)

6. the _____ paw   (tiger)

7. my _____ farm   (sister)

8. your _____ best friend   (brother)

9. our _____ advice   (mother)

10. the _____ gym   (school)

11. my _____ apple   (teacher)

12. that _____ fur   (cat)

13. the _____ teeth   (dinosaur)

14. the _____ coach   (team)

B. Write each of the phrases below in a shorter way.

1. the friend of Amanda   Amanda's friend _____

2. the car of the friend   _____

3. the keeper of the zoo   _____

4. the roar of the lion   _____

5. the cage of the tiger   _____

Plural Possessive Nouns

> - To form the possessive of a plural noun ending in -s, add only an apostrophe.
>   EXAMPLES: the boys' coats, the books' covers
> - To form the possessive of a plural noun that does not end in -s, add an apostrophe and -s.
>   EXAMPLES: men's suits, children's toys

A. Complete the chart below. You may wish to check the spellings in a dictionary.

Singular noun	Plural noun	Singular possessive	Plural possessive
1. horse	horses	horse's	horses'
2. bird			
3. teacher			
4. child			
5. truck			
6. doctor			
7. man			
8. church			

B. Rewrite each sentence using a possessive noun.

1. The cat of the Smiths has three kittens.

_____

2. The names of the kittens are Frisky, Midnight, and Puff.

_____

3. The dogs of the neighbors are very playful.

_____

4. The pen of the dogs is in the yard.

_____

5. The curiosity of the cats might get them into trouble.

_____

> ■ A **verb** is a word that shows action. The verb may show action that can be seen.
> EXAMPLE: Jane **opened** the door.
> ■ The verb may show action that cannot be seen.
> EXAMPLE: Mary **thought** about it.

A. Underline the verb in each sentence.

1. Several years ago people <u>started</u> recycling materials.
2. Today people recycle many things.
3. They buy special containers to sort their wastes.
4. In years past, few people recycled.
5. People threw most of their trash away.
6. Some people burned their trash.
7. This harmed the environment.
8. Then groups of people asked companies to recycle used materials.
9. Today many companies recycle materials.
10. People throw less trash away.
11. Many groups work hard to encourage recycling.
12. Responsible companies now recycle many things.

B. Complete each sentence with one of the verbs below.
Use each verb once.

believe	felt	hoped	knew	remember	studied	thought	worried

1. Yoko really _____ about the math test.
2. She _____ every day.
3. She _____ she could pass the test.
4. During the test, Yoko _____ carefully about each problem.
5. Could she _____ all she had studied?
6. She _____ more confident once the test was over.
7. She _____ that she had done well.
8. When Yoko got her test back, she couldn't _____ she got an A!

Helping Verbs

> ■ A verb may have a **main verb** and one or more **helping verbs**. Such a verb is called a **verb phrase**.
> EXAMPLES: The bells **were ringing**. Where **have** you **been hiding**?

A. Underline each main verb. Circle each helping verb. Some verbs do not have a helping verb.

1. (Have) you <u>heard</u> of Casey Jones?

2. He was born John Luther Jones in Cayce (Kay' see), Kentucky.

3. As a railroad engineer, he could make sad music with his locomotive whistle.

4. Soon people were telling stories about Casey.

5. One of the stories was about his train wreck.

6. One day he had climbed into his engine cab.

7. The train was carrying the mail.

8. It had been pouring rain for more than a week.

9. The railroad track was covered with water.

10. They were running late.

11. But maybe they could make it on time!

12. Around a curve, they saw a passenger train.

13. Everyone jumped.

14. But Casey did his job, faithful and true to the end.

15. People still sing about this brave railroad man.

B. Complete each sentence by adding <u>have</u>, <u>will</u>, or <u>would</u>.

1. Marla and Ricardo _____ like to go swimming.

2. They _____ received permission from their parents.

3. This _____ be their second trip to the pool today.

Present and Past Tense

> ■ A verb in the **present tense** shows an action that happens now.   EXAMPLE: I **watch** TV.
> ■ A verb in the **past tense** shows an action that happened in the past.   EXAMPLE: I **watched** TV.

A. Underline each verb in the present tense.

1. A famous poem tells about another Casey.
2. This Casey plays baseball.
3. His great skill with the bat makes him a hero.
4. The people in the town of Mudville call him the Mighty Casey.
5. Casey is one of the greatest players.
6. He frightens pitchers.
7. He often hits the winning run for his team.
8. The fans love Casey.

B. Underline each verb or verb phrase in the past tense.

1. The game had reached the last inning.
2. The Mudville team trailed four to two.
3. The first two batters were called out at first base.
4. Many in the crowd left the game and went home.
5. But the next two men up made hits.
6. Then Casey came up to the plate.
7. The crowd went wild.

C. List four verbs you know.

present tense	past tense
1.	
2.	
3.	
4.	

Future Tense

> ■ A verb in the **future tense** shows an action that will happen at some time in the future. The helping verb <u>will</u> is used with the present tense form of the verb.
> EXAMPLE: I **will meet** you tomorrow.

A. Write a verb in the future tense to complete each sentence.

1. Sue _____ the invitations.

2. David and Andrew _____ what games to play.

3. We all _____ the balloons with air.

4. Mary and Ella _____ the table decorations.

5. Carlos and Rosa _____ the cake.

6. Chris _____ of a way to get Tony to come over.

7. We all _____ in the back room.

8. When Chris and Tony come in, everyone _____, "Surprise!"

B. The sentences below show an event that happened in the past. Rewrite each underlined verb to change the event to a time in the future.

1. Carla <u>sent</u> a letter to the Round-the-World Travel Agency. ____will send____

2. She <u>received</u> an answer in a day or two. _____

3. The agency <u>mailed</u> her folders containing information about exciting places to visit. _____

4. Carla <u>studied</u> the Information. _____

5. She <u>chose</u> to write about three places. _____

6. Then she <u>planned</u> an imaginary trip to those three places. _____

7. She <u>wrote</u> in detail about her imaginary trip. _____

8. She <u>designed</u> her report with pictures from the travel agency folders. _____

9. She <u>made</u> an interesting cover for her report. _____

10. Then she <u>hoped</u> for a good grade. _____

> - A **singular subject** must have a **singular verb**.
>   EXAMPLES: Jane **lives** there. She **does walk** to school.
>   She **doesn't live** near me.
> - A **plural subject** must have a **plural verb**.
>   EXAMPLES: Jane and her sister **live** there. They **do walk**
>   to school. They **don't live** near me.
> - You and I must have a plural verb.

- **Write S over each singular subject. Write P over each plural subject. Then underline the correct verb in parentheses.**

1. Many stories (tell, tells) how dogs become friends of people.

2. A story by Rudyard Kipling (say, says) that Wild Dog

   agreed to help hunt and guard in exchange for bones.

3. After that, Wild Dog (become, becomes) First Friend.

4. Many dogs never (leave, leaves) their masters.

5. In another story, a dog (doesn't, don't) leave his master's

   dead body and dies in the Arctic cold.

6. There are few people in history that (doesn't, don't)

   record the usefulness of dogs.

7. Diggings in Egypt (prove, proves) that the dog was a

   companion in ancient Egypt.

8. Bones of dogs (does, do) appear in Egyptian graves.

9. Ancient Greek vases (picture, pictures) dogs on them.

10. Today the Leader Dog organization (train, trains) dogs

    to guide people who can't see.

11. One man who can't see said, "My eyes (have, has) a wet nose."

12. A dog (does, do) have excellent hearing and smelling abilities.

13. What person (doesn't, don't) agree that a dog is a

    person's best friend?

Agreement with Linking Verbs

- A **linking verb** is a verb that joins the subject of a sentence with a word in the predicate.

    EXAMPLES: Bob **is** an artist. Bob **was** late.
- A singular subject must have a singular linking verb.

    EXAMPLES: Maria **is** a singer. Maria **was** happy.
- A plural subject must have a plural linking verb.

    EXAMPLES: Becky and Lynn **are** sisters. The sisters **were** happy.
- <u>You</u> must have a plural linking verb.

A. Write S over each singular subject. Write P over each plural subject. Then circle the correct linking verb.

1. Tracy (is, are) a clown.

2. Her brothers (is, are) acrobats.

3. Tracy and her brothers (was, were) in a show.

4. Tracy (was, were) funny.

5. Her brothers (was, were) daring.

6. The people watching (was, were) delighted.

7. Tracy (was, were) amusing with her big red nose.

8. Tracy's brothers (was, were) high in the air on a swing.

9. (Was, Were) you ever at their show?

10. Tracy (is, are) glad that I went to see her perform.

B. Circle the correct linking verb in parentheses.

1. Ice skating (is, are) a popular winter sport today.
2. (Isn't, Aren't) there a skating rink or pond in every northern town?
3. Even in many southern towns, there (is, are) an indoor rink.
4. The discovery of ice skating (were, was) an accident.
5. An Arctic settler who slipped on a piece of bone and skidded across the ice (was, were) the inventor of the ice skate.
6. Pieces of bone attached to his feet (was, were) the first ice skates.
7. Now we (is, are) all able to enjoy his invention.
8. That (was, were) a lucky day for all ice skaters!

> ■ Never use a helping verb with <u>went</u>, <u>did</u>, <u>saw</u>, or <u>sang</u>.
>   EXAMPLES: Sue **did** her work. Sam **went** home. Sarah **sang** a song.
> ■ Always use a helping verb with <u>gone</u>, <u>done</u>, <u>seen</u>, or <u>sung</u>.
>   EXAMPLES: Sarah **has done** her work. Mary **had** not **seen** me.

A. Circle the correct verb in parentheses.

1. The class members (did, done) very well on their music project.

2. Most of them had (gone, went) to extra practices.

3. They (sang, sung) at the special spring concert.

4. The class had (sang, sung) in the concert before, but they (did, done) even better this year.

5. The teacher said she had never (saw, seen) a class work so well together.

6. The teacher said they had (sang, sung) beautifully.

7. They (sang, sung) so well that she was very proud of them.

8. The week after the concert, the class (gone, went) to a music museum.

9. The trip was a reward because the class had (did, done) so well.

10. The class (saw, seen) pictures of famous musicians at the museum.

11. After they had (saw, seen) an exhibit of unusual music boxes, they wished the boxes were for sale.

12. What do you think the teacher (did, done)?

13. She took the class to a music shop she had (gone, went) to before.

14. The teacher and the shop owner had (sang, sung) together.

15. They had (gone, went) to the same music school.

16. So the class (went, gone) to this shop and saw many little musical toys.

17. In the shop they (saw, seen) many small music boxes.

B. Write the correct form of each verb in parentheses.

1. (go)   Kate has _____ to voice class.

2. (do)   She has _____ that every day for a year.

3. (see)   Her friends have _____ her sing in public.

4. (sing)   She _____ last week at the auditorium.

Forms of *Break, Drink, Take,* and *Write*

> - Never use a helping verb with <u>broke</u>, <u>drank</u>, <u>took</u>, or <u>wrote</u>.
>   EXAMPLES: Kim **broke** her arm. Jack **wrote** a letter.
> - Always use a helping verb with <u>broken</u>, <u>drunk</u>, <u>taken</u>, or <u>written</u>.
>   EXAMPLES: Kim **has broken** her arm. Jack **had written** a note.

A. Complete each sentence with the correct form of one of the verbs below.

broke, broken   drank, drunk   took, taken   wrote, written

1. Rick _____ his time writing the letter.

2. He had _____ Janet's sculpture from her, and he needed to

   apologize.

3. He _____ slowly and carefully, thinking hard about each word.

4. Whenever he paused, he _____ sips of water from the glass on
   his desk.

5. In the letter, he said he was sorry he had _____ the sculpture.

6. Although he tried to be careful, he _____ it.

7. He _____ that he would never do anything like that again.

8. Then he read what he had _____ .

9. He saw that he had _____ all of his water.

10. It had _____ all his courage to write that letter.

B. Write the correct form of each verb in parentheses.

1. (take)   Alan had _____ his dog for a long walk and was thirsty.

2. (drink)   So he had _____ a glass of fruit juice.

3. (break)   He was careful and had not _____ the glass.

4. (break)   But then his dog, Ruby, had _____ it.

5. (write)   Now Alan has _____ a note of apology.

Forms of *Eat, Draw, Give,* and *Ring*

- Never use a helping verb with <u>ate</u>, <u>drew</u>, <u>gave</u>, or <u>rang</u>.
    EXAMPLES: Ann **ate** her lunch. The telephone **rang.**
- Always use a helping verb with <u>eaten</u>, <u>drawn</u>, <u>given</u>, or <u>rung</u>.
    EXAMPLES: Ann **has eaten** her lunch. The telephone
    has rung.

A. Complete each sentence with the correct form of the verb in parentheses.

1. (give)   Martha _____ samples of the granola bars she had made to three of her friends.

2. (eat)   The bars were soon _____, and there were cries of "More!"

3. (eat)   "You _____ those already?" Martha asked.

4. (give)   "I should have _____ you the recipe."

5. (eat)   "Please do!" said her friends. "We have never _____ anything so delicious."

6. (give)   "I _____ them to you for your health's sake," said Martha.

7. (ring)   Just then the telephone _____ .

8. (draw)   "Hello," said Martha. "You have _____ my name?"

9. (draw)   "They _____ my name as the winner!" she told her friends.

10. (ring)   "If that phone hadn't _____ when it did, we would have gone home," said Paul.

11. (eat)   "If you had _____ any faster, you would have missed all the excitement," said Martha.

B. Circle the correct verb in parentheses.

1. The telephone has just (rang, rung).

2. Carla and Betty have (eat, eaten) breakfast and are looking for something to do.

3. Now Joseph has (gave, given) them a call to ask if they would like to come to his house.

> ■ Never use a helping verb with <u>began</u>, <u>fell</u>, <u>stole</u>, or <u>threw</u>.
>   EXAMPLES: Sue **began** to run. José **fell** down.
> ■ Always use a helping verb with <u>begun</u>, <u>fallen</u>, <u>stolen</u>, or <u>thrown</u>.
>   EXAMPLES: Sue **had begun** to run. José **had fallen**.

A. Circle the correct verb in parentheses.

1. Spring baseball practice had just (began, begun).

2. The pitchers on the Blasters' team had (threw, thrown) a few balls.

3. The other Blasters (began, begun) to practice.

4. They would need much practice, because they had (fell, fallen) into last place at the end of last season.

5. The Blasters' coaches (threw, thrown) themselves into their work.

6. The biggest job (fell, fallen) on the batting and base-running coach.

7. The team batting average had (fell, fallen) out of sight.

8. And the players had (stole, stolen) only forty bases last year.

9. The coach said, "Our team motto will be 'We have just (began, begun) to fight!' "

10. With that, the Blasters (fell, fallen) to work.

11. The pitchers (threw, thrown) many different kinds of pitches.

12. The fastest pitch was (threw, thrown) at ninety miles per hour.

13. The batters were hitting everything that was (threw, thrown) to them.

B. Write the correct form of each verb in parentheses.

1. (steal)   In last night's opening game, Nick, our team's fastest

   base runner, had _____ home.

2. (begin)   We had _____ to warm up Willis, our relief pitcher,

   before the sixth inning.

3. (throw)   He had _____ the ball so well last year that

   no batters could hit his pitches.

4. (begin)   After Willis won last night's game for us, we told him that

   he had _____ our season in great style.

Subject and Object Pronouns

- A **pronoun** is a word that is used in place of a noun.
  EXAMPLES: Juan read a story. **He** enjoyed the story.
- A **subject pronoun** is a pronoun that is used as the subject of a sentence. <u>He</u>, <u>I</u>, <u>it</u>, <u>she</u>, <u>they</u>, <u>we</u>, and <u>you</u> are subject pronouns.
  EXAMPLES: **She** helped Joe. **I** helped, too.
- An **object pronoun** is a pronoun that is used in place of a noun that receives the action of the verb. <u>Her</u>, <u>him</u>, <u>it</u>, <u>me</u>, <u>them</u>, <u>us</u>, and <u>you</u> are object pronouns.
  EXAMPLES: Diane called **me**. I answered **her**.

A. Circle the subject pronoun that could be used in place of the underlined subject.

1. <u>Susan</u> (Her, She) saw the bus nearing the corner.
2. <u>Joseph</u> (Him, He) ran down the street to stop the bus.
3. <u>The children</u> (Them, They) saw Susan from the bus windows.
4. <u>Ann</u> (Her, She) called to Ms. Thomas, the driver, to wait.
5. <u>The bus</u> (It, He) stopped just in time.
6. <u>Ms. Thomas</u> (Her, She) let Susan on the bus.
7. Then <u>Susan</u> (her, she) waved goodbye to Joseph.
8. <u>Susan</u> (Her, She) was glad the bus had waited for her.

B. Circle the correct object pronoun that could be used in place of the underlined object.

1. "Tony invited Bill and (I, me) to his birthday party,"
   said <u>Tom</u>.
2. "He asked <u>Tom and Bill</u> (us, we) to be right on time,"
   Bill said.
3. "Tony's friends are giving <u>Tony</u> (he, him) a special
   gift," Tom said. "They are giving him tickets to the
   baseball game."
4. "They bought <u>the tickets</u> (them, they) last week."
5. Bill asked, "Do you think Tony's friends bought <u>Tony,
   Bill, and Tom</u> (us, we) front row seats?"
6. "Let's ask <u>Tony's friends</u> (them, they)," Tom answered.

- A **possessive pronoun** is a pronoun that shows who or what owns something.
  EXAMPLES: The shoes are **mine.** Those are **my** shoes.
- The possessive pronouns <u>hers</u>, <u>mine</u>, <u>ours</u>, <u>theirs</u>, and <u>yours</u> stand alone.
  EXAMPLES: The dog is **mine.** This book is **yours.**
- The possessive pronouns <u>her</u>, <u>its</u>, <u>my</u>, <u>our</u>, <u>their</u>, and <u>your</u> must be used before nouns.
  EXAMPLES: **Their** house is gray. **Her** cat is white.
- The pronoun <u>his</u> may be used either way.
  EXAMPLES: That is **his** car. The car is **his.**

A. Circle the possessive pronoun that completes each sentence.

1. Carol lent me (her, hers) sweater.

2. I thought that (her, hers) was warmer than mine.

3. We often trade (our, ours) jackets and sweaters.

4. I hope I don't forget which are (her, hers) and which are (my, mine).

5. My cousin Patty and I have the same problem with (our, ours) bikes.

6. Both of (our, ours) are the same make and model.

7. The only difference is that (mine, my) handlebar grips are blue and (her, hers) are green.

8. What kind of dog is (your, yours)?

9. (Your, Yours) dog's ears are pointed.

10. (It, Its) tail is stubby.

B. Complete each pair of sentences by writing the correct possessive pronoun.

1. Bill owns a beautiful horse named Tony.

   _____ spots are brown and white.

2. Bill has taught the horse some tricks.

   In fact, _____ horse counts with its hoof.

3. Bill's sisters have horses, too.

   Bill is going to train them for _____ sisters.

> ■ An **adjective** is a word that describes a noun or a pronoun.
>   EXAMPLE: The field is dotted with **beautiful** flowers.
> ■ Adjectives usually tell **what kind, which one,** or **how many.**
>   EXAMPLES: **tall** trees, the **other** hat, **five** dollars

A. In the sentences below, underline each adjective and circle the noun it describes. Some sentences may contain more than one adjective. Do not include a, an, or the.

1. The early Greeks thought a healthy body was important.

2. They believed that strong bodies meant healthy minds.

3. The Olympics began in Greece in the distant past.

4. The great god Zeus and the powerful Cronus both wanted to own Earth.

5. They battled on the high peaks of the beautiful mountains of Greece.

6. Zeus won the mighty struggle, and the first Olympics were

   held in the peaceful valley below Mount Olympus.

B. Expand the meaning of each sentence below by writing an adjective to describe each underlined noun.

1. The _____ runners from _____ nations lined up for the race.

2. Several _____ skaters competed for the _____ medal.

3. The _____ skiers sped down the _____ slopes.

4. We noticed the _____ colors of their _____ clothing against the _____ snow.

5. Hundreds of _____ fans greeted the _____ winners of each event.

6. As the _____ song of the winner's country was played, _____ tears streamed down her _____ face.

C. Fill in each blank with an adjective telling how many or which one.

1. _____ days of vacation

2. the _____ race

3. the _____ row of desks

4. _____ library books

Adjectives That Compare

- Adjectives that compare two nouns end in **-er**.
  EXAMPLES: Jack is **taller** than Bill. Bill is **heavier** than Jack.
- Adjectives that compare more than two nouns end in **-est**.
  EXAMPLE: Sam is the **tallest** and **heaviest** in the class.
- Most longer adjectives use **more** and **most** to compare.
  EXAMPLES: **more** beautiful, **most** beautiful

- **Underline the correct form of the adjective.**

   1. Last year's science fair was the (bigger, biggest)
      one we have ever had.

   2. For one thing, it had the (larger, largest)
      attendance ever.

   3. Also, most students felt that the projects were
      (more interesting, most interesting) than last year's.

   4. Of the two models of the solar system, Ray's was the
      (larger, largest).

   5. However, Mary's model was (more accurate, most
      accurate) in scale.

   6. The judges had a difficult task, but they gave the
      (higher, highest) rating to Mary's model.

   7. Sue's, Tim's, and Becky's projects on cameras drew
      the (bigger, biggest) crowds at the fair.

   8. These projects were the (more popular, most popular) of all.

   9. Sue's project had the (prettier, prettiest) display of
      photographs.

  10. But Becky's showed the (greater, greatest) understanding of
      a camera's workings.

  11. Tim's project, however, was the (finer, finest) all-around
      project of the three.

  12. One judge said, "This was the (harder, hardest)
      job I've ever had."

> - An **adverb** is a word that describes a verb. It tells **how, when, where,** or **how often** the action shown by a verb happens.
> - Many adverbs end in -ly.
>   EXAMPLES: The bell rang **loudly**. The bell rang **today**.
>   The bell rang **downstairs**. The bell rang **often**.

A. Circle each verb. Then underline each adverb that describes the verb. Next, write how, when, where, or how often.

1. Rob and Jeff (had talked) <u>daily</u> about visiting the empty old house. _____how often_____

2. They often walked by it on their way to school. _____

3. But they seldom had time to stop. _____

4. They suddenly decided that today was the day. _____

5. So on the way home from school, they slipped quietly through the front gate. _____

6. They crept carefully up the creaky front steps. _____

7. Rob quietly opened the front door. _____

8. Jeff then peered into the darkness of the front hall. _____

9. A draft of wind instantly swept through the house. _____

10. The back door banged loudly. _____

11. Rob and Jeff ran swiftly out the front door and through the gate. _____

12. They never returned to that empty old house. _____

B. Choose the correct adverb for each sentence.

finally	late	nervously	Suddenly

1. Dean's plane was arriving _____.

2. Nancy kept glancing _____ at the clock in the airport.

3. _____ the gate lights flashed.

4. Dean's plane _____ had landed.

Adverbs That Compare

> - Add -er when using short adverbs to compare two actions.
>   EXAMPLE: Joe ran **faster** than Jill.
> - Add -est when using short adverbs to compare more than two actions.
>   EXAMPLE: Jim ran **fastest** of all.
> - Use more or most with longer adverbs and with adverbs that end in -ly when comparing two or more than two actions.
>   EXAMPLES: Rob answered **more quickly** than Sue. Tim answered **most quickly** of all.

- **Complete each sentence below by writing the correct form of the adverb shown in parentheses.**

1. (close)   Amy lives _____ to Lake Hope than we do.

2. (early)   She usually arrives there _____ than we do.

3. (fast)   Amy says that I can row _____ than anyone else on the lake.

4. (quickly)   But my cousin Jake can bait a hook _____ than I can.

5. (patiently)   Amy can wait _____ than Jake and I put together.

6. (carefully)   Jake and I are both careful, but Amy baits the hook _____.

7. (quietly)   Jake and I try to see who can sit _____.

8. (soon)   I usually break the silence _____ than Jake.

9. (skillfully)   I'd have to admit that Amy fishes _____ of the three of us.

10. (happily)   And no one I know welcomes us to her home _____ than she does.

Adjectives or Adverbs

> - Remember that adjectives describe nouns or pronouns. Adjectives tell **what kind, which one,** or **how many.**
>   EXAMPLES: **blue** sky, **this** year, **several** pages
> - Remember that adverbs describe verbs. Adverbs tell **how, when, where,** or **how often.**
>   EXAMPLES: Walk **slowly.** Go **now.** Come **here.**

- **In the sentences below, underline each adjective. Circle each adverb.**

1. Three men were given licenses to hunt once on rugged Kodiak Island.

2. They had finally received permission to hunt the wild animals that live there.

3. Their purpose was different than the word "hunt" usually suggests.

4. The men were zoo hunters and would try to catch three bear cubs.

5. The young cubs would soon have a comfortable, new home at a distant zoo.

6. Once on the hilly island, the hopeful men quietly unpacked and then lay down for six hours of rest.

7. The next day, the men carefully scanned the rocky cliffs through powerful glasses.

8. They saw a huge brown bear with three cubs tumbling playfully around her.

9. The men spent two hours climbing quietly up to a point overlooking that ledge.

10. A large den could barely be seen in the rocks.

11. The wise men knew that bears never charge uphill.

12. However, the human scent immediately warned the watchful mother bear.

13. With a fierce roar, she walked heavily out of the cave and stared up at the men with her beady eyes.

14. One of the men tightly tied a red bandana and a dirty sock to a rope and threw the bundle down the slope.

15. The curious bear charged clumsily after it.

16. Quickly the men dropped to the wide ledge below.

17. But the wise cubs successfully hid from the men.

> - A **preposition** is a word that shows the relationship of a noun or a pronoun to another word in the sentence.
>   EXAMPLES: The cat **under** the tree is mine.
> - Some prepositions include: in, down, to, by, of, with, for, and at.
> - A **prepositional phrase** is a group of words that begins with a preposition and ends with a noun or a pronoun.
>   EXAMPLES: **in** the house, **down** the street, **to** us

A. Underline the prepositional phrase in each sentence below. Circle the prepositions.

1. The box ⓞⓝ the dining room table was wrapped.
2. A friend of Marta's was having a birthday.
3. Marta had been saving money for weeks so she could buy the present.
4. Now Marta was dressing in her bedroom.
5. Marta's little sister Tina toddled into the dining room.
6. She pulled the tablecloth, and the box fell to the floor.
7. Marta heard a thump and ran to the dining room.
8. Tina hid under the table.
9. The playful look on her face made Marta smile.

B. Underline ten prepositional phrases in the paragraph below.

When I went into the store, I looked at coats. I needed a new one to wear during the winter. I left my old one on the bus. When I got on the bus, I noticed it was very hot. I took off my coat and put it under my seat. When I got off the bus, I forgot it. When I asked about it, I was told to look at the office. It was not there.

C. Give directions for a treasure hunt. Use the prepositional phrases below in your sentences.

around the corner	near the school	under a rock	beneath the tree

_____

_____

_____

_____

> - <u>May</u> expresses **permission.**
>   - EXAMPLE: **May** I go to town?
> - <u>Can</u> expresses the **ability** to do something.
>   - EXAMPLE: She **can** play well.
> - <u>Good</u> is an adjective. It tells **what kind.**
>   - EXAMPLE: My sister is a **good** cook.
> - <u>Well</u> is an adverb. It tells **how.**
>   - EXAMPLE: Did you do **well** today?

- **Underline the correct word in each sentence below.**

1. (Can, May) I use the pen on your desk, Sam?
2. Yes, you (can, may) use it, but I doubt that you (can, may) make it work, Sara.
3. Look, Sam! It's working (good, well) now.
4. That's (good, well). How did you make it work?
5. (Can, May) we have an early appointment, Doctor Morris?
6. Just a moment. I'll see whether I (can, may) arrange that.
7. Yes, I believe that will work out (good, well).
8. Thank you, doctor. That will be (good, well) for my schedule, too.
9. Juan, (can, may) we have these stacks of old magazines?
10. Of course you (can, may), Shelly.
11. Are you sure you (can, may) carry them, though?
12. I (can, may) help you if they are too heavy for you.
13. Thank you, Juan, but I'm sure that I (can, may) manage very (good, well).
14. That's a (good, well) money-making project you have. What is the money being used for?
15. We're raising money for new school band uniforms, and we're doing quite (good, well), too.
16. Susan did a (good, well) job on her science project.
17. She did so (good, well) that she will take her project to the state fair this summer.
18. She will also bring a guest with her, and she has a (good, well) idea who she will bring.
19. If Alan (can, may), he will do a project and go with her.

- Teach means "to give instruction to others."
  EXAMPLE: Rosa will **teach** me to speak Spanish.
- Learn means "to get knowledge."
  EXAMPLE: I'm **learning** to speak Spanish.
- Set means "to place something in a special position."
  EXAMPLE: Please **set** the books on the table.
- Sit means "to take a resting position."
  EXAMPLE: Please **sit** down and rest for a minute.

- **Underline the correct word in each sentence below.**

1. Andy: Who will (learn, teach) you to play the piano?

2. Pat: I hope to (learn, teach) from my sister, Beth.

3. Andy: Wouldn't it be better to have Ms. Hill (learn, teach) you?

4. Pat: You were quite small when she began to (learn, teach) you.

5. Pat: Was it hard to (learn, teach) when you were so young?

6. Andy: Yes, but Ms. Hill let me (set, sit) on a high, round stool.

7. Andy: At home I would (set, sit) a thick book on the piano bench
   and (set, sit) on it.

8. Andy: Then I grew enough so that I could (set, sit) on the bench
   and still reach the keys.

9. Liz: Beth asked Marty to (learn, teach) her how to drive.

10. Liz: She says it would make her nervous to have someone that
    she didn't know (learn, teach) her.

11. Tom: Are you going to go along and (set, sit) in the back seat?

12. Liz: I doubt that Beth will want me to (set, sit) anywhere
    near when she is driving.

13. Scott: Martha, I am going to (learn, teach) you a new skill.

14. Scott: I know you are old enough to (learn, teach) how
    to (set, sit) the table.

15. Scott: (Set, Sit) there, Martha, so that you can watch me.

16. Scott: First I (set, sit) the plates in their places.

17. Scott: Then I put a glass at each place where someone will (set, sit).

18. Scott: Once I (learn, teach) you everything, you will be able
    to (set, sit) the table every night.

19. Martha: Good! Let me try to (set, sit) it now.

A. Write each noun, pronoun, verb, and adjective from the sentences below in the proper column.

1. Kathy found Ray's black science notebook.
2. She gave it to him on Thursday.
3. He was thankful.

NOUNS	PRONOUNS	VERBS	ADJECTIVES
_____	_____	_____	_____
_____	_____	_____	_____
_____	_____	_____	_____
_____	_____	_____	_____

B. Underline each verb or verb phrase in the present tense. Circle each verb or verb phrase in the past tense. Then write the future tense of each verb.

1. On that television series, we study people of other lands. _____

2. On the first program, we learned about the people of Egypt. _____

3. Old records tell us that the people plowed with a crooked stick. _____

4. They grew crops in the sand. _____

5. Some farmers raised wheat and barley. _____

C. Circle the correct verb in parentheses.

1. The parakeet had (sang, sung) in its cage all day.
2. Marilyn had (saw, seen) it do this before.
3. Once when she had (gone, went) out, she returned to find it singing.
4. The bird (did, done) its best singing in the afternoon.
5. Marilyn looked out the window and (seen, saw) why.
6. Another bird (sang, sung) back to her parakeet.

D. Write the correct form of the verb in parentheses.

1. (eat)   Rosa had just _____ breakfast.

2. (break)   Suddenly, the window in the living room _____ .

3. (fall)   Rosa almost _____ out of her chair in surprise.

4. (begin)   She had _____ to get up when she heard another noise.

5. (throw)   It sounded as though somebody had _____ something in the window.

6. (give)   She _____ the police a call.

7. (steal)   They asked if anything was _____ .

8. (write)   They _____ down the information she gave them.

9. (take)   Soon they had _____ down everything she knew.

10. (drink)   Rosa _____ a glass of water and waited for them to come.

E. Underline each prepositional phrase. Circle each adverb.

1. The police arrived shortly at Rosa's house.

2. They closely inspected the window and went around the house.

3. Rosa excitedly told them that she was too upset by it.

4. They quietly assured her that she was safe in her house.

5. Rosa could not have been more relieved by their words.

6. She waved happily at the officers as they left the scene of the crime.

F. Circle the correct word in each sentence below.

1. James (sit, set) his tape recorder on the table.

2. "I didn't know it would be so hard to (learn, teach) a new language," he said.

3. "I hope I (may, can) understand Spanish by the time we leave for Mexico."

4. "You have always been a (well, good) student," said Phillip.

5. "I hope you will (learn, teach) me some things, too."

6. "Believe me," said James, "if I (teach, learn) it (good, well) enough, I will (set, sit) you down and (teach, learn) you what I know.

A. Underline the correct word in each sentence below.

1. Someone who can't see (doesn't, don't) have to depend on another person.
2. Dog trainers (can, may) teach dogs to be their dependable guides.
3. These dogs leave (their, theirs) kennels at ten weeks of age.
4. Each puppy stays in a 4-H club (members, member's) home.
5. One member, Karen, had (her, hers) puppy, Koko, for twelve months.
6. Karen had always (wanted, will want) a puppy to take care of.
7. But, Karen had to realize that Koko was not really (her, hers).
8. "Koko and (I, me) hated to say goodbye," Karen said.
9. "It was hard to tell which one of us was (sadder, saddest)."
10. Karen had (learned, taught) Koko to walk on a leash and to display normal, (good, well) behavior.
11. The kennel owner said Karen had done her job (good, well).
12. He knew that Koko could now (learn, teach) to guide someone who can't see.
13. Now Karen (goes, went) to the kennel every week to visit Koko.
14. She has (took, taken) a treat for him each time, and Koko always wags his tail to say thank-you.
15. Koko is (largest, larger) each time Karen sees him.

B. Read the paragraph below. Find and underline the eight errors in grammar and usage. In the space above the sentences, write the correction.

The state of Kentucky is called the Bluegrass State because of

its bluish-colored grass. Rivers form a large part of Kentuckys

borders. The Ohio River is one of the longer rivers of any

in the United States. Kentucky also have many natural lakes.

Spring is the rainier season, and fall is the driest season.

Louisville are Kentucky's larger city. Louisville is the home

of the famous horse race, the Kentucky Derby.

Louisville has the name of King Louis XVI of France.

Him helped during the American Revolution. All around,

Kentucky is one of the prettier of our fifty states.

C. In the paragraph below, underline each adjective. Circle each adverb.

The circus is an exciting show to see. It has been called "The Greatest Show on Earth." Smiling children walk happily with their parents into the huge tent. They find seats quickly because the brass band is starting to play. The colorful parade will begin in three minutes. First comes the ringmaster in his bright red coat and tall hat, parading importantly to the center ring.

D. Complete this paragraph about the circus by writing adjectives or adverbs in the blanks.

Next the _____ band plays _____. The _____ bareback riders follow. Their horses walk _____. They help their riders keep their balance. Next are the _____ elephants. Each walks _____ with a _____ young rider sitting on its _____ head. The tigers snarl _____ as they pace around in their _____ cages. Everyone wants to see the _____ clowns do their _____ tricks.

E. Write the correct possessive form of each noun in parentheses.

1. (play)   The _____ subject is family life.

2. (actors)   All of the _____ parts are as family members.

3. (children)   Two of the _____ roles are played by real brothers.

4. (parent)   One _____ job takes her out of town a great deal.

5. (audience)   The _____ applause lasted for five minutes.

F. Underline the correct word in parentheses in each sentence below.

1. The mystery of the play is the (harder, hardest) to solve of any mystery I've read.

2. Why does the sun shine (brighter, brightest) in that village than at the other village?

3. This play has a (more, most) surprising ending than the other play.

- **Capitalize** the first word of a sentence.
    EXAMPLE: Many people have pen pals.
- Capitalize the first word of a direct quotation.
    EXAMPLE: Jane asked, "Where does your pen pal live?"

A. Circle each letter that should be capitalized. Write the capital letter above it.

1. "have you met your pen pal?" I asked.

2. john answered, "yes, he spent the holidays with me."

3. so I've invited my pen pal to visit me.

4. he hopes to arrive in my country next June.

5. i am making many plans for his visit.

6. we're going to hike in the mountains.

- Capitalize the first word of every line of poetry.
    EXAMPLE: There was a monkey climbed up a tree;
             When he fell down, then down fell he.
- Capitalize the first, last, and all important words in the titles of books, poems, stories, and songs.
    EXAMPLE: Who wrote *Little House on the Prairie?*

B. Circle each letter that should be capitalized. Write the capital letter above it.

1. there was an old woman

   lived under a hill,

   and if she's not gone,

   she lives there still.

2. if all the world were water,

   and all the water were ink,

   what should we do for bread and cheese?

   and what should we do for drink?

3. Have you read Longfellow's poem "the song of hiawatha"?

4. We are learning the song "down by the river."

5. If you're interested in ballooning, read *up, up and away.*

6. Mike wrote a story called "a balloon ride."

> ■ Capitalize all proper nouns.
> EXAMPLES: Main Street, Germany, Atlantic Ocean, Friday, Florida, Rocky Mountains, Halloween, December, Aunt Ann, Mom, Holmes School, James
> ■ A proper adjective is an adjective that is made from a proper noun. Capitalize all proper adjectives.
> EXAMPLES: the English language, Italian dishes, French people, American tourists, the Australian cities

A. Circle each letter that should be capitalized. Write the capital letter above it.

1. My friend larry had just returned from a world trip.

2. He brought gifts for everyone in my family, including my

   dog, chipper.

3. He gave my mother some delicate japanese dishes that he

   bought in tokyo, japan.

4. He gave my sister a scottish plaid kilt like the bagpipers

   wear in scotland.

5. My father really likes the hat larry got for him in london.

6. The hat reminds us of the kind sherlock holmes wore.

7. My gift was an african drum from mali in west africa.

8. larry told us how delicious the italian food was.

9. chipper's gift was a colorful, embroidered dog jacket

   from thailand.

**B. Write four sentences about a trip you would like to take.
Use proper nouns and at least one proper adjective in the sentences.**

1. _____

2. _____

3. _____

4. _____

> ■ Capitalize a person's title when it comes before a name.
>   EXAMPLES: Mayor Thomas, Governor Swanson
> ■ Capitalize abbreviations of titles.
>   EXAMPLES: Dr. Norris; Mr. and Mrs. J. B. Benton, Jr.;
>   Ms. Harris; Mr. John F. Lynch, Sr.

A. Circle each letter that should be capitalized. Write the capital letter above it.

1. We saw governor potter and senator williams in their offices.

2. They were discussing a national health problem with dr. laura bedford and mayor phillips.

3. We ate lunch with rev. barton and mr. james adams, jr.

4. They are part of a committee planning a welcome for prince charles of England, who will tour our state next month.

> ■ Capitalize abbreviations of days and months, parts of addresses, and titles of members of the armed forces. Also capitalize all letters in abbreviations for states.
>   EXAMPLES: Mon.; Sept.; 501 N. Elm St.; Capt. W. R. Russell; Chicago, IL

B. Circle each letter that should be capitalized. Write the capital letter above it.

1. gen. david e. morgan
   6656 n. second ave.
   evanston, il 60202

2. valentine's day Exhibit
   at oak grove library
   mon.—fri., feb 10—14
   101 e. madison st.

3. sgt. carlos m. martinez
   17 watling st.
   shropshire SY7 0LW, england

4. maxwell school Field Day
   wed., apr. 30, 1:00
   Register mon.—tues., apr. 28—29
   mr. modica's office

> ■ Use a **period** at the end of a declarative sentence.
>   EXAMPLE: The lens is an important part of a camera.
> ■ Use a **question mark** at the end of an interrogative sentence.
>   EXAMPLE: Do you enjoy having your picture taken?

A. Add the correct end punctuation to each sentence below.

1. Photography is an exciting hobby for many people

2. My friend Karen is one of those people

3. Have you ever gone on a vacation with a camera bug

4. Craig and I love Karen's photos

5. But getting those really good shots can be tiring

6. Can you imagine waiting in the hot desert sun while Karen
   gets just the right angle on a cactus

7. Or have you ever sat in the car while your friend waited
   for a grazing elk to turn its head

8. I don't need so much time when I take pictures

9. Of course my pictures aren't always as good as Karen's

B. Add the correct end punctuation where needed in the paragraphs below.

Have you ever wondered what it would be like to live as
our country's pioneers did___ You can visit log homes made to
look like the original cabins of pioneer days___ Then you can
see how difficult life was for the pioneers who helped our
country grow___

The cabins were small and roughly built___ Many cabins had
just one room___ Where was the kitchen___ Most of the cooking was
done in the large fireplace___ The fireplace also supplied the
only heat___ Wasn't it cold___ You can be sure the winter winds
whistled between the logs___ And where did the pioneers sleep___
Most cabins had a ladder reaching up to the bedroom loft___

The furniture in the cabins was usually as roughly built as
the cabins themselves___ All the clothing was handmade by the
family___ They ate food grown and caught on their land___ Would
you have liked to live in those times___

> - Use a period at the end of an imperative sentence.
>   EXAMPLE: Please sign your name here.
> - Use an **exclamation point** at the end of an exclamatory sentence.
>   EXAMPLE: What a wonderful time we had at the show!

C. Add the correct end punctuation to each sentence below.

1. A group of friends decided to go ice skating___
2. Terry asked, "Is Thursday okay with all of you___"
3. Carmen said, "It sounds great to me___"
4. They all agreed to meet at the lake___
5. Elaine said, "Wow, is it ever cold___"
6. "Get moving," said Leon. "You'll warm right up___".
7. They skated for several hours___
8. Terry asked, "Who's ready to sit close to a warm fire___"
9. Carmen said, "I thought you'd never ask___"
10. Suddenly she was hit by a snowball___
11. "Hey___" she shouted. "What's the big idea___"
12. Elaine laughed and said, "It's not that cold out___"

D. Add the correct end punctuation where needed in the paragraphs below.

Have you ever seen pictures of northern Minnesota___ It is a region of many lakes___ My family once spent a week on Little Birch Lake___ What a sight it was___

There were thousands of white birches reflected in the blue water___ The fishing was great___ Every day we caught large numbers of bass, and every night we cooked fresh fish for our dinner___

The nearest town was Hackensack___ At the waterfront was a large statue of Diana Marie Kensack___ She is seated at the water's edge___ Her gaze is fixed on the horizon___ Do you know who she was___ Legends say that she was Paul Bunyan's sweetheart___ She is still waiting at the shore for him to come back to her___ Be sure to visit Diana when you are in Minnesota___

> - Use **quotation marks** to show the exact words of a speaker. Use a comma or other punctuation marks to separate the quotation from the rest of the sentence.
>   EXAMPLE: "Who made this delicious candy?" asked Claire.
> - A quotation may be placed at the beginning or the end of a sentence. It may also be divided within the sentence.
>   EXAMPLES: Lawrence said, "Let's play checkers."
>   "My brother," said Leslie, "brought me this ring."

A. Add quotation marks to each sentence below.

1. We will read about a great inventor today, said Miss Davis.

2. Let me see, Miss Davis went on, whether you can guess who the inventor is.

3. Will you give us some clues? asked Chris.

4. Yes, answered Miss Davis, and here is the first clue.

5. His inventions have made our lives easier and more pleasant, said Miss Davis.

6. Is it Alexander Graham Bell? asked Judy.

7. Mr. Bell did give us the telephone, said Miss Davis, but he is not the man I have in mind.

8. This man gave us another kind of machine that talks, Miss Davis said.

9. It must be Thomas Alva Edison and the phonograph, said Jerry.

10. You are right, Miss Davis said.

B. Place quotation marks and other punctuation where needed in the sentences below.

1. Polly asked Where will you spend the holidays, Michelle?

2. We plan to drive to Henry's ranch said Michelle.

3. Polly asked Won't it be quite cold?

4. Yes said Michelle but it will be so much fun to slide down the hill behind the house.

5. It's great fun to go into the woods and cut down a Christmas tree added Bob.

6. Come with us said Michelle.

- Use an **apostrophe** in a contraction to show where a letter or letters have been taken out.
  EXAMPLE: I **can't** be there until three o'clock.
- Use an apostrophe to form a possessive noun. Add -'s to most singular nouns. Add -' to most plural nouns.
  EXAMPLE: Mike's gym shoes are high tops. The men's suits are blue and white.

- **Write the word or words in which an apostrophe has been left out. Insert the apostrophe.**

1. Building a new homes the dream of many people.   _____home's_____

2. It can also become a persons worst nightmare.   _____

3. Cant you see that planning carefully is the key?   _____

4. If you dont plan everything, somethings bound to go wrong.   _____

5. Youd better start by finding out how many rooms youll need.   _____

6. An architects view may also be helpful.   _____

7. Getting many opinions can help you decide whats best.   _____

8. But youd better already have some idea before you begin, or you'll have problems.   _____

9. Find out everyones wishes for their rooms.   _____

10. Others ideas may be completely different from your own.   _____

11. If you talk it over, everyones ideas can be used.   _____

12. You wouldnt want to end up with a home youre completely unhappy with.   _____

13. After all, your homes the place where youll be spending most of your time.   _____

> ■ Use a **comma** between words or word groups in a series.
>   EXAMPLE: Food, medical supplies, blankets, and clothing
>   were rushed to the flooded area.
> ■ Use a comma to separate the parts of a compound sentence.
>   EXAMPLE: Many homes were flooded, and the owners
>   were taken to safety in boats.

A. Add commas where needed in the sentences below.

1. The heavy rain caused flooding in Cedarville
   Taylorville Gardner and other towns along the Cedar River.

2. The flood washed away bridges roads and some small homes.

3. Our home had water in the basement and most of our
   neighbors' homes did, too.

4. We spent the night bailing mopping and worrying.

5. We put our washer and dryer up on blocks and then we
   helped Elaine.

6. Some of our shrubs flowers and small trees may have to
   be replaced.

7. Elaine's newly-planted vegetable garden was washed
   away and the Smiths lost their shed.

8. The people in our neighborhood were very lucky and
   everyone agreed that the flood brought us closer together.

> ■ Use a comma to separate a direct quotation from the rest of
> a sentence.
>   EXAMPLE: "We're leaving now," said Ann. Ann said, "It's
>   time to go."

B. Add commas where needed in the sentences below.

1. Sally asked "Why did the rooster cross the road?"

2. "To get to the other side " answered Terry.

3. "That's really an old joke " Terry added.

4. Sally asked "Do you know a newer one?"

5. Terry asked "What holds the moon up?"

6. "Moon beams " said Terry.

- Use a comma to set off the name of a person who is addressed.
    EXAMPLE: "Alan, can't you go with us?" asked Bill.
- Use a comma to set off words like yes, no, well, and oh when they begin a sentence.
    EXAMPLE: "No, I have to visit my aunt," answered Alan.

C. Add commas where needed in the sentences below.

1. "Melody and Tim would you like to go to the hockey game?" Marie asked.
2. "Oh yes!" Tim exclaimed.
3. "Marie I'd love to," called Melody.
4. "Well it's settled," said Marie.
5. "Ted did you go to the model show last night?" asked Sam.
6. "No I couldn't make it," answered Ted.
7. "Oh I was going to ask if Carlos won a prize," Sam said.
8. "Well I hope so," Ted said.
9. "Well then," Sam said, "let's call and ask him."
10. "Carlos did you win a prize last night?" Sam asked.
11. "Yes I did," replied Carlos.
12. "Oh what did you win?" asked Sam.
13. "Well you'd never guess," answered Carlos.
14. "Carlos don't keep us guessing," said Sam.
15. "Well you know my model was of a helicopter. My prize was a ride in a helicopter!" exclaimed Carlos.

D. Pretend that you and your friends are planning an outing. Write a conversation that might take place between you and your friends. Use the names of the persons being addressed. In some sentences, use yes, no, oh, or well. Punctuate your sentences correctly.

_____

_____

_____

_____

_____

_____

A. Circle each letter that should be capitalized. Write the capital letter above it.

1. last summer we toured montana and alberta.

2. my friend bob liked hiking in the rocky mountains.

3. the trip down the snake river was my favorite part.

4. we spotted two american bald eagles.

5. i liked glacier park best.

6. bob bought a book named *tales of the old west*.

7. dr. vicenik is governor adams's personal doctor.

8. mrs. vicenik and mr. morrison are brother and sister.

9. ms. louis has invited dr. vicenik's son to speak to our group.

10. we made a poster with this information on it:

    walter vicenik will speak

    at winston school

    on tues., apr. 25 at 3:00

B. Add the correct end punctuation to each sentence below.

1. I love to walk on the beach ___

2. Look at that sunset ___

3. Have you ever seen anything so beautiful ___

4. The waves sound so soft lapping in on the sand ___

5. Take a picture of me ___

6. Shall I take one of you ___

7. Look, there's a starfish ___

8. I've never seen one before ___

9. Don't pick it up ___

10. It belongs in the sea ___

C. Add commas, quotation marks, and apostrophes where needed in each sentence below.

1. Mark do you know where George is? asked Donna.

2. No I dont answered Mark.

3. Hes supposed to meet you Kiko and me here she said.

4. Mark asked Why didnt you tell us?

5. I did! Donna exclaimed. Dont you remember our talk yesterday?

6. Oh now I do said Mark.

7. Donna said Ill bet George didnt remember.

8. Heres Kiko. At least she remembered and shes ready to help plan the fund-raiser said Donna.

9. Oh Im sure George will be here said Mark.

10. Hes always ready to meet new people talk and help others out.

D. Correct the letter below. Circle each letter that should be capitalized. Add missing commas, periods, quotation marks, and apostrophes. Be sure to write the correct end punctuation on the blank after each sentence.

955 s rimfire

clayton mo 64645

aug 25 2006

dear josé

   i cant wait to see you ___ its going to be great visiting mexico city ___ i know its now one of the largest cities in the world ___ i cant imagine such a huge place ___

   when i went to see dr fulton for my shots, he said eric my boy dont worry about anything ___ mexico is a wonderful place to visit ___ ive been there many times and always enjoyed myself ___

   i said dr fulton did you ever get lost trying to find your way around ___ he said he hadnt but he also always had a good guide ___ im glad ill have you there to show me around ___

   honestly josé youve got to know how exciting this is ___ i want to see everything do everything and learn everything i can about your country ___

                   your friend

                   eric

A. Correct the story below. Circle each letter that should be capitalized. Add missing periods, question marks, exclamation points, commas, quotation marks, or apostrophes where needed. Be sure to write the correct end punctuation on the blank after each sentence.

have you ever read eugene fields poem, "the duel"___
The chinese plate and the old dutch clock told the story
to a poet___ they were hanging above the fireplace and
they could see the gingham dog and the calico cat sitting
on the table___

the gingham dog said bow-wow-wow___

mee-ow answered the calico cat___

then the dog and the cat began to fight___ bits of gingham
and calico were scattered everywhere___

the chinese plate cried oh what can we do___
but the dog and cat continued to tumble and fight all night___
the next morning there was no trace of dog or cat___

many people said burglars must have stolen them___
but the old chinese plate said to the poet they ate each
other up and thats the truth___

what a surprise ending that was___

B. Make corrections in the story below as you did in Exercise A.

There is a russian folktale named "the coming of the snow
maid___" it tells about winter in russia where winter is very
long and very cold___

ivan, a peasant, and his wife, marie, had no children___ they
often watched their neighbors children at play in the snow___
one day marie got an idea___

ivan lets make a snow child she said___ we can pretend
it is our own___

the snow child came alive and they called her Snow Maid___
she grew rapidly until early june___ then she disappeared
in a tiny cloud___

dont cry marie said ivan___ Snow Maid has returned to the
sky but she will come back to us next september___

C. Correct the story below. Circle each letter that should be capitalized. Write the capital letter above it. Add missing periods, commas, quotation marks, or apostrophes where needed. Be sure to write the correct end punctuation on the blank after each sentence.

A World War II hero, general dwight david eisenhower, became

president eisenhower___ in his youth, he was just one of

six eisenhower boys___ he and his brothers, arthur edgar earl

roy and milton, grew up on the edge of abilene, kansas___

All the boys had chores to do, morning noon and night___ One

of the older brothers chores was to push the youngest brothers

baby buggy___ dwight, or ike, as he was called, would

lie on the floor while reading a book, and push and

pull the buggy back and forth with his feet___

his mother once said ike was good at hoeing___ he hoed the

garden of beans peas potatoes corn cabbage carrots and

beets___ the boys went to lincoln school she said and always played

baseball in the schoolyard___ she often had to patch ikes pants

as a result of his sliding into home plate___

all the brothers liked to read___ ike enjoyed greek and

roman history and stories about military leaders___ his

high school classmates thought he would become a history

teacher at yale university___

D. Write a paragraph about one of our national heroes or someone you know and admire. Follow all the rules of capitalization and punctuation.

_____

_____

_____

_____

_____

- Every sentence has a base. The **sentence base** is made up of a simple subject and a simple predicate.
  EXAMPLE: <u>Men</u> <u>stared</u>.
- Add other words to the sentence base to expand the meaning of the sentence.
  EXAMPLE: The **bewildered** men stared **in amazement at the mysterious light**.

A. Expand the meaning of each sentence base below. Add adjectives, adverbs, and/or prepositional phrases. Write your expanded sentence.

1. (Plane flew.) _____

2. (Creatures ran.) _____

3. (Dogs played.) _____

4. (Police chased.) _____

5. (Boys discovered.) _____

**B. Imagine two different scenes for each sentence base below.
Write an expanded sentence to describe each scene you imagine.**

1. (Children explored.) a. _____

   b. _____

2. (Fire was set.) a. _____

   b. _____

3. (Crowd roared.) a. _____

   b. _____

4. (Wind blew.) a. _____

   b. _____

5. (Friend sent.) a. _____

   b. _____

6. (Actor was dressed.) a. _____

   b. _____

> ■ A **topic sentence** is a sentence that states the main idea of a paragraph.   EXAMPLE: **Many of the best things in life are free.** The sun and the moon give their light without charge. A true friend can't be bought. The beauty of the clouds in a blue sky is there for all to enjoy.

A. Write a topic sentence for each of the paragraphs below.

1.   The summer had been extremely hot and dry. Many brush fires had broken out. People were told not to water their lawns or wash their cars. People responded by using less water and being careful about how they used water. Everyone realized the new rules were in the best interest of everyone.

TOPIC SENTENCE: _____

2.   Nancy read everything she could find about nursing. She spent hours in the library learning about first aid. When the call came for summer volunteers at the hospital, she was the first to sign up. She was determined to prepare herself as best she could for what she hoped would be her career.

TOPIC SENTENCE: _____

3.   There are many parks to enjoy. Museums and aquariums have interesting exhibits. Large stores and malls have a great selection of things to buy. Many large cities also have major sports teams to watch.

TOPIC SENTENCE: _____

B. Choose one of the topics below. Write a topic sentence for it. Then write a paragraph of about fifty words in which you develop the topic.

The most useful invention   My favorite holiday

A frightening experience   A place I want to visit

_____

_____

_____

_____

_____

_____

- Sentences that contain **supporting details** develop the topic sentence of a paragraph. The details may be facts, examples, or reasons.

A. Read the topic sentence below. Then read the numbered sentences. Underline the four sentences that contain details that support the topic sentence.

TOPIC SENTENCE: Automobile seat belts save lives.

1. The first seat belts didn't have shoulder straps.

2. A seat belt helps keep a front-seat passenger from going through the windshield.

3. A passenger who doesn't fasten his or her seat belt may be hurt if the car is in an accident.

4. Seat belts protect small children from falls and bumps while riding in the back seat.

5. Some cars have automatic seat belts.

6. Studies on the number of lives saved prove the value of wearing seat belts.

B. Underline the correct word to complete the sentence.

The supporting details in the sentences above were (facts, examples, reasons).

C. Choose one of the topic sentences. Write it on the first line. Then write three sentences that contain supporting details. The details may be facts, examples, or reasons.

1. Having a pet is a lot of work.

2. A large (or small) family has advantages.

3. My vacation (in the mountains, at camp, on the seashore, or other place) was fun.

4. Every student should have an allowance.

_____

_____

_____

_____

D. Fill in the blank below with the word <u>facts</u>, <u>examples</u>, or <u>reasons</u>.

The supporting details in my paragraph were _____.

> ■ **Comparing** two objects, persons, or ideas shows the likenesses between them. Comparing expresses a thought in a colorful, interesting way.
>   EXAMPLE: Walking lets the walker be as free as a bird that has flown from its cage.
> ■ **Contrasting** two objects, persons, or ideas shows the differences between them. Contrasting can also express a thought in a colorful, interesting way.
>   EXAMPLE: Baby Rachel's morning mood is one of sunshine, rainbows, and laughter. Her nap-time mood, however, suggests gathering clouds.

A. Read each topic sentence and the pair of sentences that follow. Underline the sentence that expresses a supporting detail in a colorful, interesting way.

1. TOPIC SENTENCE: Having the flu is no fun.

   a. Pat was tired of being in bed with the flu.

   b. After a week in bed with the flu, Pat felt like her pet hamster, Hamby, spinning his wheel in his cage.

2. TOPIC SENTENCE: Koalas aren't all they seem to be.

   a. A koala is cute but unfriendly.

   b. A koala looks like a cuddly teddy bear, but it is about as friendly as a grizzly bear.

B. Rewrite each sentence below in a more colorful, interesting way. Use comparison or contrast.

1. A mosquito bite is itchy.

   _____

2. Taking a bus to a museum is fun.

   _____

3. Dogs are friendlier than cats.

   _____

4. Reading is a good way to spend your free time.

   _____

5. Stealing a base makes baseball exciting.

   _____

Lesson 55

Using Location

> ■ Supporting details can be arranged in order of location.
>   EXAMPLE: The sofa was **on the long wall to your right.**
>   A table sat **at either end** of the sofa.

A. In the paragraph below, underline the words that show location.

    I stood watching. <u>Below me</u> was the ball field. Across the street from the ball field, men were building an apartment house. Cement trucks were lined up along the street. They were delivering concrete for the basement walls of the apartment house. A kindergarten class was playing baseball on the ball field. The wise teacher told the class to move away from the street.

B. Choose one of the scenes or objects below. Write a topic sentence about it. Then write a paragraph of at least five sentences describing the scene or object. Use words such as <u>above</u>, <u>ahead</u>, <u>around</u>, <u>behind</u>, <u>next to</u>, <u>on top of</u>, and <u>under</u> to show location.

    Scenes: your street, your home, a garden

    Objects: your bicycle, a car, your favorite book

_____

_____

_____

_____

_____

_____

_____

_____

_____

_____

C. Underline the words you used to show location.

> - The **topic** of a paragraph should be something the writer is interested in or familiar with.
>   EXAMPLES: school, animals, science, sports, hobbies
> - The **title** should be based on the topic.
> - The **audience** is the person or people who will read what is written.
>   EXAMPLES: classmates, readers of the class newspaper, family members

A. **Suppose that the topic chosen is <u>sports</u>. Underline the sports topic below which you would most like to write about.**

1. Is winning the most important thing in sports?

2. There are many reasons why tennis (or baseball, or

   swimming, or ____) is my favorite sport.

3. Sports can be an enjoyable family activity.

B. **Think about the topic you underlined in Exercise A. Underline the audience below that you would like to write for.**

1. your family

2. a coach

3. your best friend

C. **Write a paragraph of about seventy words, using the sentence you underlined in Exercise A as your topic sentence. Write a title for your paragraph. Direct your paragraph to the audience you underlined in Exercise B.**

_____

_____

_____

_____

_____

_____

_____

_____

_____

Lesson 57

Clustering

■ **Clustering** uses a special drawing that shows how ideas relate to one main topic. That topic is written in a center shape. Other shapes contain the ideas. Lines show how the ideas are connected to the main topic.

EXAMPLE:

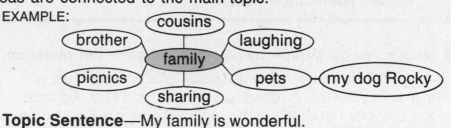

Topic Sentence—My family is wonderful.

A. Complete each cluster below by writing words that the topic makes you think of. You may add additional shapes and connecting lines.

1.

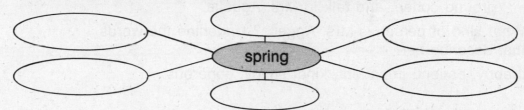

TOPIC SENTENCE: _____

2.

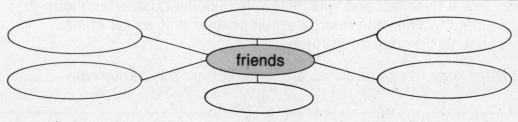

TOPIC SENTENCE: _____

B. Choose one of the topics in Exercise A. Write it on the title line below. Then write your topic sentence for that topic. Complete the paragraph.

_____

_____

_____

_____

_____

_____

> ▪ A **descriptive paragraph** describes something. It is made colorful and interesting through the use of details.
>   EXAMPLE: A **thick coating** of dust covered everything in the **old abandoned** house.

A. Read the descriptive paragraph below. Then answer the question.

   In my neighborhood, there is a small grocery store just a block from my house. A retired couple, Mr. and Mrs. Aggens, are the owners. I always hope that Mrs. Aggens will wait on me. She is friendly and full of smiles. She always gives me extra large scoops of ice cream. She doesn't hurry me when I can't decide whether to spend my money on apples or fruit bars. After I make my purchase, I like to stay, smell the freshly ground coffee, and talk to Mrs. Aggens.

1. What kind of person is Mrs. Aggens? Underline the words that describe her.

crabby, patient, impatient, kind, stingy, generous

B. Read the paragraph below about the same store.

   In my neighborhood, there is a store near our house. The owners are a husband and wife. The wife is patient, generous, and friendly. Near the door is a fruit counter and an ice cream counter. I often shop there.

1. List at least five details that are missing from this paragraph. _____

_____

_____

2. What is the result of leaving out these details? _____

_____

C. Write a descriptive paragraph about a place you visit often. Use details to make your paragraph colorful and interesting.

_____

_____

_____

_____

> - Writers use **descriptive words** that tell how something looks, feels, smells, tastes, or sounds.
>   EXAMPLE: The **shady** forest was dressed in the **soft greens** and **pale yellows** of early spring.
> - Writers use verbs that tell exactly what someone is doing or how someone moves.
>   EXAMPLE: Richard **tramped** across the newly mopped kitchen floor.

A. Read the paragraph below, and answer the questions that follow.

>   Jody stood silently at the rickety gate of Harry's weathered old ranch house. The crooked gate hung on only its top hinge. The house that had never known a paintbrush seemed to have whitened with age. A gentle breeze rippled the tall grass and filled Jody's nostrils with the sugary smell of sweet peas. Jody turned. Yes, there were those lovely white, pastel pink, and lavender blooms. But everything else had faded with age.

1. What words tell how the ranch house looked? _____

how the gate looked? _____

2. What word tells how the breeze felt? _____

how the grass looked? _____ how it moved? _____

how the sweet peas smelled? _____ how they looked? _____

B. Choose a familiar place to write about in a descriptive paragraph. Write a topic sentence to begin the paragraph. Think about how the place looks, the sounds you might hear there, the smells you might smell there, how it feels to be there, and the things you might taste there. Write descriptive sentences that tell about these things to complete your paragraph.

_____

_____

_____

_____

_____

Revising and Proofreading

> - **Revising** gives you a chance to rethink and review what you have written and to improve your writing. Revise by adding words and information, by deleting unneeded words and information, and by moving words, sentences, and paragraphs around.
> - **Proofreading** involves checking spelling, punctuation, grammar, and capitalization. Use proofreader's marks to show changes needed.

Proofreader's Marks

=	⊙	SP
Capitalize.	Add a period.	Correct spelling.
/	∧	¶
Make a small letter.	Add something.	Indent for new paragraph.
∧	℘	⟶
Add a comma.	Take something out.	Move something.

A. Rewrite the paragraphs below. Correct the errors by using the proofreader's marks.

¶ during the history of Earth, there have been several ice ages, these were times when giant sheets of ice spred across many parts of earth. People think that almost one third of the Land was covered by these hug sheets of ice.

The last ice age frozed so so much ocean water that the level of the oceans dropped. then lots of land apeared that usually lay underwater When the tempeture began to warm up the ice sheets melted. The Ocean levels rose again.

_____

_____

_____

_____

_____

_____

A. Expand the meaning of each sentence base below. Add adjectives, adverbs, and/or prepositional phrases. Write the expanded sentences.

1. (Reporter wrote.) _____

2. (Pilot flew.) _____

3. (Dentist drilled.) _____

4. (Crowd cheered.) _____

B. Write a topic sentence for the paragraph below.

    A car engine needs a radiator to stay cool. A radiator is a tank with

thousands of openings for air to pass through. As the engine runs, hot

water travels through hoses to the radiator. As the car moves, air cools the

hot water in the radiator. When the car is stopped or moving slowly, a fan

forces more air into the radiator.

TOPIC SENTENCE: _____

C. Read the topic sentence below. Then underline the three sentences that contain details supporting the idea of the topic sentence.

TOPIC SENTENCE: Many unique animals live in rain forests.

1. It is very hot in a rain forest.

2. Squirrel monkeys live in the rain forests of Central and South America.

3. Parrots and toucans sit in the trees and eat fruits and nuts.

4. I would like to see a rain forest.

5. Flying squirrels glide from tree to tree.

D. Write three supporting details for the following topic sentence. In the blank before each sentence, tell whether each is a fact, example, or reason.

TOPIC SENTENCE: There is too much violence on television today.

_____ 1. _____

_____ 2. _____

_____ 3. _____

E. Read the descriptive paragraph below. Then answer the questions.

From the window of the seaplane, Lucy spotted the island. It looked like an emerald in the middle of a shining turquoise sea. She immediately forgot the thundering sound of the propellers and the bouncy ride that she feared would give her a pounding headache. A sudden spray of sea water on the window startled her. As the plane drifted gently toward land, Lucy could almost smell the sea air. Bright pink and red flowers lined the sidewalks.

What words describe:

1. what the island looked like from the plane? _____

2. the sea? _____

3. the propellers? _____

4. how the plane moved toward land? _____

5. what color the flowers were? _____

6. how the plane ride was? _____

7. what Lucy thought her headache might become? _____

8. the sea water on the window? _____

F. Rewrite the paragraph below. Correct the errors by following the proofreader's marks.

¶ soils come in in two basic types. they are clay or sandy. Heavy soil, or clay, has small partikles that don't allow much air in. Sandy Soil is made of bigger pieces, and this tipe of soil pervides lots of of air for plant roots. You should carfully study the soil type of you have befor you plant anything.

_____

_____

_____

_____

_____

_____

A. Complete the cluster below. Write a title for the topic. Then write a topic sentence and three sentences that contain supporting details.

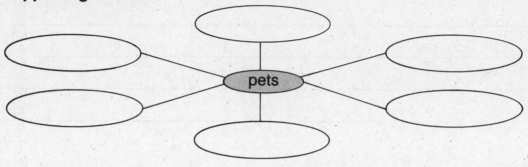

TOPIC SENTENCE: _____

_____

_____

_____

B. Write a paragraph of at least four sentences describing your living room, kitchen, or bedroom. Use location words such as <u>above</u>, <u>ahead</u>, <u>around</u>, <u>behind</u>, <u>next to</u>, <u>on top of</u>, and <u>under</u>.

_____

_____

_____

_____

C. Fill in the blanks in the paragraph below with descriptive words and action verbs that make the paragraph colorful and interesting.

The _____ colt pulled itself up on its _____

legs. Then it _____ after its mother. Just as the colt

neared the fence, a _____, _____ rabbit

_____ under the fence and _____ up to the colt.

The startled colt _____ and let out a _____ neigh.

Its _____ mother _____ up to its side _____.

D. Choose one of the topic sentences below. Write a paragraph of four sentences, using <u>reasons</u> to support the thought of the topic sentence.

   1. Everyone should learn to swim.
   2. Laws are necessary.
   3. Summer vacations are just the right length of time.

_____

_____

_____

_____

E. Choose one of the topic sentences below. Write a paragraph of four sentences, using <u>examples</u> to support the thought of the topic sentence.

   1. Many television programs are educational.
   2. Electrical inventions have made our lives easier.
   3. A hobby is more than a way to take up time.

_____

_____

_____

F. Read the paragraph below. Use proofreader's marks to revise and proofread the paragraphs. Then write your revised paragraph.

try to imagine what the world would be like if there were

no People in it. There would be no cities towns or

villages There would be no bildings of any knind. nobody

would be be there to do or make Anything.

_____

_____

_____

_____

_____

_____

> ■ When following written **directions,** it is important to read each step carefully. Be sure you have completed one step before going on to the next step.

■ **Read the recipe below. Then answer the questions that follow it.**

Peanut Butter Balls

½ cup wheat germ   ½ cup powdered milk
½ cup sunflower seeds   ½ cup honey
½ cup peanut butter   ½ cup sesame seeds (if desired)

a. Spread wheat germ and sunflower seeds on a cookie sheet. Bake at 350° for 15 minutes, stirring every 5 minutes.

b. Place toasted wheat germ and sunflower seeds in a bowl.

c. Add all other ingredients except sesame seeds. Mix well.

d. Form into balls, using 1 teaspoonful of dough for each ball.

e. Roll balls in sesame seeds. (This step is not necessary.)

f. Chill for 3 hours.

g. Serve as a tasty, good-for-you snack or dessert.

1. What is the recipe for? _____

2. What kitchen utensils are needed? _____

3. What quantity of each ingredient is needed? _____

4. What ingredients are used in step a? _____

5. What should the oven temperature be? _____

6. How long should the wheat germ and sunflower seeds
   be baked? _____

7. How often should you stir the wheat germ and sunflower seeds
   while they are baking? _____

8. How much dough is needed to form each ball? _____

9. How long should the peanut butter balls be chilled before
   eating? _____

10. Which ingredient may be left out? _____

- **Alphabetical order** is used in many kinds of listings.
  EXAMPLE: Miss Clark's class list: Adams, Coss, Edwards, Gutierrez, Lee, Ortega, Shapiro, Turner

A. Complete each sentence below.

1. The letter <u>n</u> comes after _____ and before _____ .

2. The letters between <u>s</u> and <u>w</u> are _____ .

- Entries in a dictionary or an encyclopedia appear in alphabetical order, according to their first letters, second letters, third letters, and so on.
  EXAMPLE: wave, wax, web, weed, wish, wisp

B. Number the words in each group in alphabetical order.

    3   4   2   1

1. whale, where, weary, water   3. earth, ease, each, earn

2. school, second, safety, sailor   4. recess, rain, ring, rose

C. Number the encyclopedia entries in each column in alphabetical order.

1. _____ Bell, Alexander Graham   1. _____ Panda

2. _____ Berlin   2. _____ Pago Pago

3. _____ Bear   3. _____ Panama Canal

- Names in a telephone book are listed in alphabetical order, according to last names. When several people have the same last name, their names are arranged in alphabetical order, according to first names.   EXAMPLE: Barnes, John; Barnes, William; Barton, Clyde; Barwin, James D.

D. Copy the names in the order you would find them in a telephone book.

T. C. Caskey   _____   Cindy Lyons   _____

Louis J. Caskey   _____   Paul Lyndale   _____

Dictionary: Guide Words

■ **Guide words** are words that appear at the top of each page in a dictionary. They show the first and last entry words on the page. Guide words tell whether an entry word is listed on that page. EXAMPLE: **beets/beyond:** The word <u>begin</u> will appear on the page. The word <u>bid</u> will not.

A. Read each pair of guide words and the list of entry words below. Put a check in front of each entry word that would appear on the page.

1. blade/bluff

_____ blur   _____ blast

_____ blink   _____ black

_____ blame   _____ blaze

_____ blossom   _____ blunder

_____ blush   _____ blouse

2. intend/island

_____ into   _____ invent

_____ instrument   _____ isn't

_____ introduce   _____ irrigate

_____ iron   _____ itch

_____ inward   _____ invite

B. Read each pair of guide words and the list of entry words below. Circle only the entry words that would appear on the page. Then write those words in the order in which they would appear in the dictionary.

1. meal/minister

meanwhile _____

melody _____

meadow _____

mention _____

mischief _____

2. product/provide

professor _____

propeller _____

proceed _____

program _____

protest _____

3. rear/rescue

recess _____

realize _____

recognize _____

reckon _____

receive _____

4. miserable/mitten

mist _____

mischief _____

miss _____

mite _____

mixture _____

- A **syllable** is each part of a word that is pronounced at one time.
- Dictionary entry words are divided into syllables to show how to divide a word at the end of a writing line.
- Put a **hyphen** (-) between syllables when dividing a word.
  EXAMPLE: a-wak-en

- **Find each word in a dictionary. Write the word, placing a hyphen between syllables.**

1. chemical ___chem-i-cal___
2. gasoline _____
3. degree _____
4. marvelous _____
5. disappear _____
6. chimney _____
7. continent _____
8. miserable _____
9. generally _____
10. glacier _____
11. arithmetic _____
12. exercise _____
13. hospital _____
14. problem _____
15. window _____
16. language _____
17. agriculture _____
18. parakeet _____
19. beginning _____
20. simple _____

21. determine _____
22. musician _____
23. salary _____
24. cheetah _____
25. interrupt _____
26. dentist _____
27. recognize _____
28. rascal _____
29. innocent _____
30. educate _____
31. achievement _____
32. darling _____
33. homestead _____
34. calendar _____
35. missionary _____
36. farewell _____
37. aluminum _____
38. bacteria _____
39. program _____
40. banana _____

Lesson 65 — Dictionary: Pronunciation

- Each dictionary entry word is followed by a respelling that shows how the word is **pronounced,** or said.
- **Accent marks** (′) show which syllables are said with the most stress.   EXAMPLE: au-to-mat-ic (ô′ tə mat′ ik)
- A **pronunciation key** (shown below) explains the other symbols used in the respelling.

A. Answer the questions below about the respelling of the word <u>automatic</u>. Use the pronunciation key at the right. (ô′ tə mat′ ik)

1. What is a key word for the symbol <u>ô</u>? _____

2. What is a key word for the symbol ə? _____

3. What is the key word for the symbol <u>a</u>? _____

4. What is the key word for the symbol <u>i</u>? _____

> at; āpe; fär; câre; end; mē; it; īce; pîerce; hot; ōld; sông; fôrk; oil; out; up; ūse; rüle; pu̇ll; tûrn; chin; sing; shop; thin; <u>th</u>is; hw in white; zh in treasure. The symbol ə stands for the unstressed vowel sound in about, taken, pencil, lemon, and circus.

B. Use the pronunciation key as you look at each respelling. Underline the word for which the respelling stands.

1. (ə ban′ dən)   ability   abandon   aboard
2. (bak′ strōk′)   backstop   bakery   backstroke
3. (klench)   clef   clench   clerk
4. (dān′ tē)   daisy   dainty   dance
5. (hīt)   height   hit   hint
6. (en tīr′ lē)   entirely   entry   entertain
7. (wi<u>th</u>′ ər)   whether   withhold   wither
8. (noiz)   nosy   noise   nose
9. (ôt)   out   at   ought
10. (wāt)   wit   white   weight
11. (wal)   wall   walk   wail
12. (vizh′ ən)   vision   visible   visit
13. (frāt)   free   fright   freight
14. (our)   hope   hour   ours
15. (dī′ mənd)   demand   diamond   dime
16. (sat′ əl īt′)   satisfy   salary   satellite
17. (mī′ grāt)   mighty   migrate   migrant
18. (ang′ gəl)   angry   angle   anger

> - A dictionary lists the **definitions** of each entry word. Many words have more than one definition. Sometimes a definition is followed by a sentence showing a use of the entry word.
> - A dictionary also tells the **part of speech** for each entry word. An abbreviation (shown below) stands for each part of speech.
>   EXAMPLE: **aunt** (ant, änt) *n.* **1.** the sister of one's father or mother. **2.** the wife of one's uncle.

A. Use the dictionary sample below to answer the questions.

au-di-ence (ô′ dē əns) *n.* **1.** a group of people gathered in a place to hear or see, such as those watching a movie at the theater. **2.** an opportunity of being seen or heard; hearing: *He will explain as soon as he has an audience.* **3.** a formal meeting with someone of importance: *The committee will serve as your audience so that you can present your plan.* **4.** people who enjoy and support something: *Baseball has a large audience in America.*

au-di-o-vis-u-al (ô′ dē ō vizh′ ōō əl) *adj.* **1.** the type of materials that aid in teaching or learning through the use of both hearing and sight. **2.** of or relating to hearing and sight.

au-di-to-ri-um (ô′ də tôr′ ē əm) *n.* **1.** a large hall in a school, church, or other public building. **2.** a room or building used for large, public gatherings.

au-di-to-ry (ô′ də tôr′ ē) *adj.* of, relating to, or experienced through hearing.

1. How many definitions are given for the word

   audience? _____ for the words audiovisual and

   auditorium? _____ for the word auditory? _____

2. Which part of speech does the abbreviation n.

   stand for? _____

3. Which part of speech is audiovisual and

   auditory? _____

4. Which words in the dictionary sample are

   nouns? _____

n.	noun
pron.	pronoun
v.	verb
adj.	adjective
adv.	adverb
prep.	preposition

B. Write the number of the dictionary definition used for the underlined word.

1. _____ At the end of the movie, the audience clapped loudly to show how much they had enjoyed it.

2. _____ All the Olympic gold medal winners were given an audience with the President.

3. _____ The prisoner asked for an audience with the prison officials.

Parts of a Book

> - The **title page** tells the name of a book and the name of its author.
> - The **copyright page** tells who published a book, where it was published, and when it was published.
> - The **table of contents** lists the chapter or unit titles and the page numbers on which they begin. It is at the front of a book.
> - The **index** gives a detailed list of the topics in a book. It gives the page numbers for each topic. It is at the back of a book.

A. Answer the questions below.

1. Where should you look for the page number of a particular topic? _____

2. Where should you look to find out who wrote a book? _____

3. Where should you look to find the name of a book? _____

4. Where should you look to find out who published a book? _____

5. Where should you look to get a general idea of the contents of a book? _____

6. Where should you look to find out when a book was published? _____

B. Use your *Language Exercises* book to answer the questions.

1. What is the title of this book? _____

2. On what page does Unit Five start? _____

3. List the pages that deal with revising and proofreading. _____

4. What is the copyright date of this book? _____

5. Who are the authors of this book? _____

6. On what page is the lesson on writing topic sentences? _____

7. Where is the index? _____

8. On what page does Unit Two start? _____

9. List the pages that deal with prepositions. _____

10. What lesson is on page 43? _____

- An **encyclopedia** is a reference book that has articles on many different subjects. The articles are arranged in alphabetical order in different books, called volumes. Each volume is marked to show which subjects are inside.
- **Guide words** are used to show the first subject on each page.
- There is a listing of **cross-references** at the end of most articles to related subjects that the reader can use to get more information on that subject.

A. Read the sample encyclopedia entry below. Use it to answer the questions that follow.

WATER is a liquid. Like air (oxygen), water is necessary for all living things. A person can live only a few days without water. Water is lost from the body every day and must be replaced. Drinking and eating replace water. About 60 percent of a person's body weight is water. *See also* OXYGEN.

1. What is the article about? _____

2. Why is water important? _____

3. How much of a person's body is water? _____

4. How is water in the body replaced? _____

5. What other subject could you look under to get more information? _____

6. What could be another related topic? _____

OXYGEN is a gas that has no smell, no taste, and no color. Nearly all living things need oxygen to live. Oxygen mixes with other things in a person's body to produce energy needed for life processes. Oxygen is also an important part of water. Oxygen is sometimes called air.

7. How are oxygen and water the same? _____

8. Does the above cross-reference mention water? _____

9. How does the article describe oxygen? _____

10. What is another word for oxygen? _____

> - When looking for an article in the encyclopedia:
>   Look up the last name of a person.
>   EXAMPLE: To find an article on Babe Ruth, look under <u>Ruth</u>.
>   Look up the first word in the name of a city, state, or country.
>   EXAMPLE: To find an article on New York City, look under
>   <u>New</u>.
>   Look up the most important word in the name of a general
>   topic.
>   EXAMPLE: To find an article on the brown bear, look under
>   <u>bear</u>.

B. Write the word you would look under to find an article on each of the following subjects.

1. Susan B. Anthony _____

2. salt water _____

3. New Mexico _____

4. lakes in Scotland _____

5. Rio de Janeiro _____

6. United Kingdom _____

7. modern literature _____

8. breeds of horses _____

C. The example below shows how the volumes of one encyclopedia are marked. The volumes are numbered. The subjects are in alphabetical order. Write the number of the volume in which you would find each article.

A	B	C-CH	CI-CZ	D	E	F	G	H	I-J	K
1	2	3	4	5	6	7	8	9	10	11

L	M	N	O	P	Q-R	S	T	U-V	W-Z
12	13	14	15	16	17	18	19	20	21

_____ 1. caring for chickens

_____ 2. the flag of the United States

_____ 3. how glass is made

_____ 4. vitamins

_____ 5. reptiles

_____ 6. the history of Japan

_____ 7. how rainbows are formed

_____ 8. pine trees

Review

A. Read the directions below. Then answer the questions that follow.

Take Highway 72 north to the Elm Street exit. Turn left, and cross the highway. Go to the first stop sign, beside the school. Turn right on Bluffside, and go to the second stoplight. Turn left. Go one block, and then turn right on Creekway. Peter's address is 1809 Creekway. His house is blue and sits at the top of the hill on the left.

1. Where do these directions take you? _____

2. How many left turns will you take? _____

3. What street is Peter's house on? _____

4. Which direction do you go on Highway 72? _____

5. What sign is by the school? _____

B. Use the sample dictionary page below to answer the questions that follow.

traffic / transatlantic

traf-fic (traf′ ik) *n.* **1.** people, automobiles, ships or similar objects coming and going along a route or way of travel: *There was a lot of traffic at the ballpark after the game.* **2.** buying and selling, especially for profit; an exchange of goods. **3.** dealing in something improper or illegal: *Our government is trying to stop the drug traffic in our country.* **4.** the business done by a transportation system.

tram-ple (tram′ pəl) *v.*, **tram-pled, tram-pling,** to stomp on; stamp with the foot; tread on so heavily as to crush or injure.

trance (trans) *n.* **1.** a condition somewhat like sleep, as that produced by hypnotism. **2.** a dreamy or stunned state: *He sat in a trance, dreaming of his summer vacation.*

tran-quil (trang′ kwəl) *adj.* calm; peaceful; free from disturbance. —**tran′ quil-ly, adv.**

trans-at-lan-tic (trans′ ət lan′ tik) *adj.* **1.** that which crosses or extends across the Atlantic Ocean: *They made a transatlantic telephone call.* **2.** on the other side of the Atlantic Ocean.

1. What are the guide words? _____

2. Which word is a verb? _____ How is its pronunciation shown? _____

3. Which words are nouns? _____

_____

4. Which word has the most syllables? _____

5. Which word has only one syllable? _____

6. Which words are adjectives? _____

7. Which word means "to stomp on"? _____

8. What is the meaning of <u>tranquil</u>? _____

_____

C. Use the sample encyclopedia entry to answer the questions.

> **Lock** Locks are sets of gates that help ships move through canals. Each lock is on a different level, and two sets of gates make up each lock. The locks are similar to stairs. A ship moves into a lock, and the gates in front of and behind the ship close. Water is then pumped into or let out of the enclosed lock. This raises or lowers the ship to the level of the next lock. *See also* CANAL.

1. What is the article about? _____

2. What do locks do? _____

3. How many sets of gates does a lock have? _____

4. What are locks compared to in the article? _____

5. What is the cross-reference? _____

D. The example below shows how the volumes of a small encyclopedia are marked. Circle the word you would look under to find an article on each of the following subjects. Then write the number of the volume in which you would find each article.

A–C	D–F	G–H	I–L	M–N	O–R	S–T	U–W	X–Z
1	2	3	4	5	6	7	8	9

_____ 1. the history of mining   _____ 5. the capital of Sweden

_____ 2. Mark Twain   _____ 6. Great Danes

_____ 3. the Nile River   _____ 7. Japanese gardens

_____ 4. plant life of the tundra   _____ 8. how volcanoes erupt

E. Write title page, copyright page, table of contents, or index to tell where to find this information.

_____ 1. the author's name

_____ 2. the page on which certain information can be found

_____ 3. the year the book was published

_____ 4. the page on which a certain chapter starts

_____ 5. the company that published the book

A. Read the recipe below. Then answer the questions that follow.

<u>Low-Calorie Buttermilk Dressing</u>

3 tablespoons lemon juice

1 1/4 teaspoons seasoned salt

1/4 teaspoon prepared mustard

1 cup buttermilk

Sugar

Combine all ingredients except sugar. Blend well. Add sugar to taste. Pour on lettuce or spinach salad. Makes 1 cup.

1. How much sugar do you use? _____

2. How much does the recipe make? _____

B. Write the words below on the lines beside their respellings and definitions.

academy   accompany

_____ **1.** (ə kad′ ə mē) **1.** a private high school.
2. a school giving training in a special field.

_____ **2.** (ə kum′ pə nē) **1.** to go along with.
2. to perform a musical accompaniment for.

C. Read the guide words. Then write the words from the box that would be found on the same page, placing a hyphen between syllables.

slop/sneer

1. _____

2. _____

3. _____

sliding	sliver
slumber	smattering
snuggle	sluggish

D. Write <u>title page</u>, <u>copyright page</u>, <u>table of contents</u>, or <u>index</u> to tell where to find this information.

_____ **1.** the chapter titles in a book

_____ **2.** the year a book was published

_____ **3.** the page number on which a topic can be found

_____ **4.** the title of a book

E. Find the article for <u>butternut</u> in an encyclopedia. Then answer the following questions.

1. What encyclopedia did you use? _____

2. What are butternuts? _____

3. What is another name for butternut? _____

4. How are butternuts used? _____

5. How do butternuts grow? _____

6. In what countries are butternuts found? _____

7. What were the husks of butternuts used for? _____

8. Why were the husks good for spinning cloth? _____

9. Why do you think the cross-references are important? _____

10. Does the article mention the cross-references? _____

F. The example below shows how the volumes of one encyclopedia are marked. Circle the word under which you would look to find an article. On the first line, write the number of the volume you would look in to find the article. Then number the subjects in alphabetical order on the second lines.

A	B	C-CH	CI-CZ	D	E	F	G	H	I-J	K
1	2	3	4	5	6	7	8	9	10	11

L	M	N	O	P	Q-R	S	T	U-V	W-Z
12	13	14	15	16	17	18	19	20	21

_____ _____ 1. the city of Springfield   _____ _____ 7. invention of the zipper

_____ _____ 2. kinds of vegetables   _____ _____ 8. life span of a monkey

_____ _____ 3. Great Wall of China   _____ _____ 9. Walt Disney

_____ _____ 4. uses for boxcars   _____ _____ 10. kinds of melons

_____ _____ 5. uses of the snowshoe   _____ _____ 11. how aspirin is made

_____ _____ 6. life cycle of the bee   _____ _____ 12. lakes in Paraguay

Synonyms, Antonyms, and Homonyms ▪ Write <u>S</u> before each pair of synonyms. Write <u>A</u> before each pair of antonyms. Write <u>H</u> before each pair of homonyms.

1. _____ kind, cruel

2. _____ stop, halt

3. _____ been, bin

4. _____ together, apart

5. _____ come, arrive

6. _____ build, destroy

7. _____ beet, beat

8. _____ take, seize

9. _____ I'll, aisle

10. _____ help, hurt

11. _____ grow, increase

12. _____ here, there

13. _____ mane, main

14. _____ locate, find

15. _____ same, different

Homographs ▪ Write the homograph for each pair of meanings below. The first letter of each word is given for you.

1. a. to be silent   b. a flower   m _____

2. a. to hit   b. a sweet drink   p _____

3. a. to be able   b. a tin container   c _____

4. a. part of the eye   b. student   p _____

5. a. to mix   b. to move around   s _____

6. a. a sharp point   b. to knock over   t _____

Prefixes and Suffixes ▪ Add a prefix or suffix from the box to the base words in parentheses. Write the new word in the blank.

re-   -ful   mis-   -less   un-   pre-   -able

1. Susan was (happy) _____ when her new computer didn't work.

2. She (read) _____ the directions.

3. She found that she had (understood) _____ them the first time.

4. It seemed the problem was (repair) _____ .

5. She was ready for a (view) _____ of what her computer could do.

6. Susan knew she would spend (end) _____ hours using it.

7. She knew her computer would be (depend) _____ .

8. She noticed that there were many (help) _____ programs on it.

Contractions ▪ **Write the two words that make up the contraction in each sentence.**

_____ _____ 1. "Let's go to the movies," said Janet.

_____ _____ 2. "We've been two nights this week," said Tim.

_____ _____ 3. "I'm just trying to catch up," said Janet.

_____ _____ 4. "They've made so many I want to see."

_____ _____ 5. Tim said, "We can't see all of them."

_____ _____ 6. "Couldn't we try?" asked Janet, laughing.

Compound Words ▪ **Use the words below to form a compound word that will complete each sentence. Write the word on the line.**

plant	water	stand	power	play	fall	mate	under

1. The beautiful _____ splashed into a clear pool below.

2. My little sister's favorite _____ is moving.

3. I couldn't _____ what he was saying.

4. The _____ produced large amounts of electricity.

Contractions and Compound Words ▪ **Underline the contractions, and circle the compound words in the paragraph. Then write each underlined or circled word and the two words from which it is made.**

I wondered what the firefighter was doing. He was standing in the roadway, but he wasn't directing traffic. I looked up, and in the treetop was a kitten. It couldn't get down. There was a woman standing by the tree. She was the owner of the kitten.

1. _____ _____

2. _____ _____

3. _____ _____

4. _____ _____

5. _____ _____

Recognizing Sentences ▪ Write $\underline{S}$ before each sentence.

1. _____ Many interesting facts about bees.

2. _____ Bees have five eyes.

3. _____ On an ounce of honey for fuel.

4. _____ Bees tell other bees the distance to pollen areas.

Types of Sentences ▪ Identify the types of sentences below by writing $\underline{D}$ before a declarative sentence, $\underline{IN}$ before an interrogative sentence, $\underline{IM}$ before an imperative sentence, and $\underline{E}$ before an exclamatory sentence.

1. _____ Did you know that there are 20,000 kinds of bees?

2. _____ There is so much to learn about bees!

3. _____ Tell me how much honey each person in the United States eats each year.

4. _____ Honey producers say the average is about one pound per person.

5. _____ Do you eat that much honey in one year?

6. _____ No, I don't, so someone must be eating my share!

Subjects and Predicates ▪ Draw a line between the subject and the predicate in each sentence below. Underline the simple subject once. Underline the simple predicate twice.

1. The honey-making industry makes about $115 million each year.

2. An average bee can fly fifteen miles in an hour.

3. A worker honeybee makes about one-tenth of a pound of honey in its lifetime.

4. Its lifetime is just one growing season.

5. Two hundred bees make about one pound of honey in one season.

6. A waxy material is released by bees.

7. This material is used in candles and polishes.

8. Bees cannot defend themselves against other insects.

9. At least one kind of fly can kill them.

10. Robber flies kill bees with their piercing beaks.

Compound Subjects and Predicates ▪ Draw a line between the complete subject and the complete predicate in each sentence. Underline each compound subject once and each compound predicate twice.

1. Planets and moons revolve around other bodies in space.

2. Mercury and Venus revolve around the sun in less than a year.

3. The nine planets in our solar system rotate and spin like tops.

Compound Sentences ▪ Write <u>C</u> before each compound sentence.

_____ 1. The dark clouds rolled in, and then it began to rain.

_____ 2. We were worried about the dogs.

_____ 3. They were outside, so we went to look for them.

_____ 4. We searched everywhere, but we couldn't find them.

_____ 5. They usually stayed home when the weather was bad.

_____ 6. Soon we heard scratching at the door.

_____ 7. We opened it, and they shook their wet coats all over us.

Run-On Sentences ▪ Separate the run-on sentences below. Rewrite them correctly on the lines.

1. Laura tried to fix her car she changed the oil, she put in a new air filter.

_____

2. It worked it ran well she had done a good job.

_____

Compound Sentences and Run-on Sentences ▪ Rewrite the paragraph. Combine simple sentences into compound sentences, and separate run-on sentences.

      Sometimes we hop in the car when we get restless. We just drive wherever we choose. It's fun and relaxing, we laugh and forget about our problems. After a while we have gone far enough, we turn around and drive back home.

_____

_____

_____

_____

Singular, Plural, and Possessive Nouns ▪ Complete the chart below. Write the forms called for in each column.

Singular Noun	Plural Noun	Singular Possessive	Plural Possessive
1. actor			
2. baby			
3. beach			
4. horse			
5. woman			
6. child			

Action Verbs and Linking Verbs ▪ Underline each verb or verb phrase in the sentences below.

1. The little Lion-Dog was once a palace guard dog in Tibet.
2. The Lion-Dog got its name because of the breed's thick, lion-like mane.
3. Today, Lhasa apso is the name of the breed.
4. Mainly a companion or a show dog, the Lhasa apso will guard its master's home.
5. Lhasa apsos gaze out a window at each person that goes by.

Using Verbs Correctly ▪ Circle the correct verb in parentheses.

1. Jake and I (is, are) friends.
2. One year we (go, went) camping with our friends.
3. We thought it (sounds, sounded) like fun.
4. We all (throw, threw) out ideas about where to go.
5. That was where the problems (begin, began).
6. We (drawn, drew) straws to decide.
7. Tom (choose, chose) the longest one, so he got to pick.
8. We decided we would (taken, take) a trip to Texas.
9. We all decided that Texas (was, were) an interesting place to visit.

Pronouns ▪ Underline each pronoun. Write S if it is a subject pronoun, O if it is an object pronoun, and P if it is a possessive pronoun.

_____ **1.** Jake, are your suitcases packed yet?

_____ **2.** I packed lots of summer clothes.

_____ **3.** They will be great to wear in Texas.

_____ **4.** Jake answered me by saying no.

_____ **5.** Then Tom said he would help Jake pack.

_____ **6.** Jake, Tom, Susan, and I finished right on time.

Adjectives and Adverbs ▪ Underline each adjective, and circle each adverb in the paragraph below.

> After several hours, Jake began to talk quietly. He wondered what the most beautiful place in Texas was. Susan said that Austin was prettier than any other city. Tom loudly disagreed. He spoke knowingly of the golden sands and blue waters of Galveston. Susan gently reminded him that it had been a long time since he had been there. His wonderful memories might not be entirely accurate.

Prepositions ▪ Underline each prepositional phrase in the sentences below. Circle each preposition.

1. Before we reached Austin, it grew hot inside the car.

2. As we traveled down the highway, we began to see changes.

3. The flat land became more hilly as we got closer to Austin.

4. We looked for signs of cowboys and ranches.

5. Our idea of Texas was influenced by the movies we had seen.

Using Words Correctly ▪ Circle the correct word in each sentence below.

1. If we (can, may), we will go all the way to the coast.

2. We are (learning, teaching) a great deal about Texas.

3. It's not easy to (set, sit) in a car for so long.

4. But it is still a (well, good) experience.

5. Seeing the big state is (learning, teaching) us we were wrong.

6. We learned that lesson very (good, well).

Capitalization ▪ Correct the sentences below. Circle each letter that should be capitalized. Write the capital letter above it.

1. i have always wanted to visit yellowstone national park.

2. jeri and i decided to go see it in march, before the crowds arrived.

3. we almost stayed in wyoming because the grand teton mountains were so beautiful.

4. cody was a wonderful town, founded by colonel william f. cody, better known as buffalo bill.

5. however, the book we were reading, *the history of the old west* by dr. e. j. james, convinced us to go on to california.

6. we stopped in las vegas, nevada, to send postcards back to our friends in missouri.

7. all jeri could talk about was seeing old faithful, the most famous geyser in the world.

8. i bought a book of black-and-white photographs by ansel adams that was magnificent.

Using Commas and End Punctuation ▪ Add commas and the correct end punctuation as needed in each sentence.

1. Yellowstone National Park was established in 1872

2. There are many hot springs in the park and wildlife is protected there

3. Moose deer antelope bear and other smaller animals are at home in the park

4. What a great variety of geysers can be seen there

5. You can enjoy canyons waterfalls lakes forests and meadows

6. Be sure to see Emerald Pool when you visit the park

7. Can you picture a hot spring colored by the blue sky

8. The Upper Falls of the Yellowstone River drop 109 feet and the Lower Falls drop 308 feet

9. What a beautiful sight the waterfall is

10. Yes Yellowstone Park is a national treasure

Using Quotation Marks and Apostrophes ▪ Add commas, apostrophes, and quotation marks as needed in each sentence.

1. Have you seen Pats new car? asked James.
2. No I havent yet said Diane.
3. What kind did he get? she asked.
4. I dont know for sure said James but I know its red.
5. Diane said How do you know that?
6. He always said thats what hed buy said James.
7. He couldve changed his mind said Diane.
8. James said Not Pat. Hes not the kind of person whod do that.
9. Well said Diane lets go see it now.
10. Lets go! said James.
11. Wow! said Diane. That's a great car!
12. Pat where did you get it? asked James.
13. I got it at the car lot downtown said Pat.

Using Capitalization and Punctuation Correctly ▪ Circle each letter that should be capitalized. Add missing commas, periods, quotation marks, and apostrophes. Be sure to write the correct end punctuation in the blank after each sentence.

1309 w. harriman st
maysville ky 40419
sept 17 2006

dear shelley

 you wont believe what happened___ we went to a melodrama, a kind of play, and i became an actor___ yes its true___ can fame and fortune be far behind___ heres what happened___ we were just sitting there ready to boo the villain when the stage manager came out and asked is there a volunteer in the audience___ before i knew what was happening, deanna had grabbed my elbow and pushed my hand into the air___ the stage manager pointed at me and said come on up here and tell us all your story___

 well i nearly fainted of course but i had no choice___ so i did it and it was the most fun ive had in a long time___ i acted out the part of a woman who refuses a heros help___ he tried to save me from paying rent to a horrible landlord but i took care of him myself___ then the hero shook my hand and rode off into the sunset___ it was so funny___ deanna has pictures and i cant wait to show them to you___

see you soon
ellen

Writing Sentences ▪ **Expand the meaning of each sentence base below. Add adjectives, adverbs, and/or prepositional phrases. Write your expanded sentences.**

1. (Geese flew.) _____

2. (Thieves robbed.) _____

3. (Winter approaches.) _____

4. (Doctors treated.) _____

Topic Sentences ▪ **Write a topic sentence for the paragraph below.**

    My dog and I play ball together. We go on hikes together. My dog is always happy to see me. My dog barks to let me know that a stranger is near. I can teach my dog to obey and to do tricks. I feed and bathe my dog.

TOPIC SENTENCE: _____

Supporting Details ▪ **Read the topic sentence below. Then underline the three sentences that contain supporting details.**

TOPIC SENTENCE: Finding an apartment takes organization.

1. Look in the newspaper ads for vacant apartments.

2. Driving all over town looking for signs on lawns takes too much time.

3. Check the address to be sure the apartment is in an area you like.

4. Make a list of questions to ask the landlord.

5. Try to remember what each person you talk to says.

Topic and Audience ▪ **Circle the audience to whom you would send a letter on each topic below.**

1. problems with a new appliance

    a. your family   b. the manufacturer   c. your friends

2. media coverage of local elections

    a. newspaper   b. the mayor   c. the governor

3. concern over rising electric rates

    a. your landlord   b. the electric company   c. your uncle

Clustering ▪ Complete the cluster by writing words that the topic in the center of the cluster relates to. On the line under the cluster, write the audience to whom you would address a paragraph about jobs.

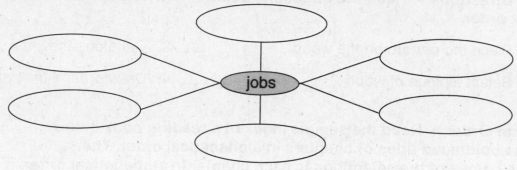

Audience: _____

Writing a Paragraph ▪ Now write a paragraph about jobs. Keep the audience you chose in mind. Write a topic sentence and three sentences that contain supporting details. The supporting details may be reasons, facts, or examples.

Jobs

_____

_____

_____

_____

_____

Revising and Proofreading ▪ Rewrite the paragraph below. Correct the errors by using the proofreader's marks.

¶Lakes are bodys of water with land all around. They do not connect to the the ocean. most lakes contain fresh water, although a few have salt water. Some very large lakes are called Seas.

_____

_____

_____

_____

Following Directions ▪ Read the directions below. Then number them in the correct order.

_____ 1. Place the pattern on the wood.   _____ 3. Cut along the lines you drew.

_____ 2. Select a piece of wood.   _____ 4. Draw around the pattern.

Alphabetical Order ▪ Read the sample index of a reading book below. Number the boldfaced titles of chapters in alphabetical order. Then number the names of the selections in each chapter in alphabetical order.

INDEX: Types of Reading

_____ **Poems**   _____ **Fiction**

_____ Limericks   _____ The Firm

_____ Sonnets   _____ All That Jazz

_____ **Stories of Real People**   _____ **Articles**

_____ Churchill, Man of His Times   _____ Violence in America

_____ The Life of Helen Keller   _____ How to Choose a Good School

Guide Words ▪ Read the guide words for a dictionary page below. Put a check before each entry word that would appear on that page.

1. eggnog / eject   **2. harbor / harp**

_____ eggplant   _____ eight   _____ harm   _____ harp

_____ eel   _____ eggbeater   _____ hare   _____ happy

Pronunciation ▪ Use the pronunciation key as you look at each respelling. Underline the word that matches

1. (sin′ dər)   sender   cinder   single

2. (nā′ shən)   navy   notion   nation

3. (härp)   harm   harp   happy

> at; āpe; fär; câre; end; mē; it;
> īce; pîerce; hot; ōld; sông; fôrk;
> oil; out; up; ūse; rüle; pu̇ll; tûrn;
> chin; sing; shop; thin; **th**is;
> hw in white; zh in treasure.
> The symbol ə stands for the
> unstressed vowel sound in
> about, taken, pencil, lemon,
> and circus.

Parts of a Book ▪ Write <u>title page</u>, <u>copyright page</u>, <u>table of contents</u>, or <u>index</u> to tell where you would find this information.

_____ 1. a chapter title

_____ 2. the page on which certain information can be found

_____ 3. the author's name

_____ 4. the year a book was published

Using an Encyclopedia ▪ Read the sample encyclopedia entry below. Use it to answer the questions that follow.

BRAN is the outer layers of food grains. When flour is made, the outer layers of grain come off. These particles are bran. Bran is a very healthful food. It is full of vitamins and minerals. Bran is used as a breakfast food and as an ingredient in baking. Pure bran is dark brown in color. Pure bran is often combined with other cereal grains, such as wheat. _See also_ FIBER and CEREAL.

1. What is the article about? _____

2. What is bran? _____

3. How is bran obtained? _____

4. What color is pure bran? _____

5. What is a grain that is often combined with pure bran? _____

6. What are the cross-references? _____

Using an Encyclopedia ▪ Circle the word you would look under to find an article on each of the following. Then write the number of the volume in which you would find each.

A–C	D–F	G–I	J–L	M–N	O–Q	R–S	T–V	W–Z
1	2	3	4	5	6	7	8	9

_____ 1. learning how to swim

_____ 2. San Antonio

_____ 3. dentistry skills

_____ 4. the life cycle of the ant

_____ 5. Harriet Tubman

_____ 6. how syrup is made

_____ 7. the cause of a yawn

_____ 8. breeds of cats

A. Write S before each pair of synonyms, A before each pair of antonyms, and H before each pair of homonyms.

_____ **1.** right, write   _____ **3.** ajar, open

_____ **2.** open, shut   _____ **4.** top, bottom

B. Write the homograph for the pair of meanings.

_____ **a.** past tense of see   **b.** a tool for cutting

C. Write P before each word with a prefix, S before each word with a suffix, and C before each compound word.

_____ **1.** redraw   _____ **3.** outside

_____ **2.** meaningful   _____ **4.** overwork

D. Write the words that make up each contraction.

_____ **1.** don't   _____ **2.** I'll

E. Write D before the declarative sentence, IM before the imperative sentence, E before the exclamatory sentence, and IN before the interrogative sentence. Then circle the simple subject, and underline the simple predicate in each sentence.

_____ **1.** Where are you going?   _____ **3.** You cannot do that!

_____ **2.** I am going down into the cave.   _____ **4.** Do not be afraid.

F. Write CS before the sentence with a compound subject. Write CP before the sentence with a compound predicate.

_____ **1.** The snow swirled and drifted.

_____ **2.** Deanne and Juan went skiing.

G. Write CS before the compound sentence. Write RO before the run-on sentence.

_____ **1.** I heard the train's whistle, it sounded far away.

_____ **2.** The train passed, but I didn't hear the whistle again.

H. Underline the common nouns, and circle the proper nouns in the sentence.

Judge Merkle sentenced Harold Jones to three years in jail for his crime.

I. Write the correct possessive noun to complete the second sentence.

The hands of the workers were cold. The _____ hands were cold.

J. Write **A** if the underlined verb is an action verb, **L** if it is a linking verb, and **H** if it is a helping verb.

_____ **1.** They <u>darted</u> in front of us.

_____ **2.** We <u>grew</u> irritated.

_____ **3.** They <u>were</u> pushing us too far.

K. Write <u>past</u>, <u>present</u>, or <u>future</u> to show the tense of each underlined verb.

_____ **1.** Soon I <u>will know</u> the question.

_____ **2.** I <u>know</u> the answer.

_____ **3.** I <u>knew</u> I was right.

L. Circle the correct verb in each sentence.
1. He (go, went) with her and (taken, took) the class.
2. They (drunk, drank) a can of juice and (begin, began) to read.
3. She had (given, gave) him some crackers, but he (thrown, threw) them away.
4. He (steal, stole) a peek at her paper and (fallen, fell) out of his chair.

M. Write **SP** before the sentence that has a subject pronoun, **OP** before the sentence that has an object pronoun, and **PP** before the sentence that has a possessive pronoun.

_____ **1.** Their daughter is grown.

_____ **2.** She lives in Los Angeles, California.

_____ **3.** Frank and Stephanie visited her last summer.

N. On the line before each sentence, write <u>adjective</u> or <u>adverb</u> to describe the underlined word.

_____ **1.** The bird chirped <u>sweetly</u>.

_____ **2.** Its <u>beautiful</u> song made me whistle.

O. In the sentence below, underline each prepositional phrase, and circle each preposition.

Under the leaves was a small kitten that had been left by its mother.

P. Circle the correct word in each sentence.

1. You (can, may) come with us.
2. Do you feel (good, well)?
3. Let me (learn, teach) you how to use a thermometer.
4. (Set, Sit) on the chair.
5. (May, Can) you read what the sign says?

Q. In the letter below, underline letters that should be capitalized, and add punctuation where needed.

908 s greenslope

st paul mn 60598

mar 11 2006

dear sara

ive finally grown to like this job ___ who wouldve dreamed that would

happen ___ do you remember how much i hated it when i got here ___

everyone said emily youll love it if you give it a chance ___ well they were

right ___

youd like it here but i know you wont come ___ write to me soon ___

your sister

emily

R. Expand the meaning of the sentence base below.

Lions roared. _____

S. Write a topic sentence and two sentences with descriptive supporting details on the topic of city living.

_____

_____

_____

T. Number the following directions in order.

_____ 1. Load the film.

_____ 2. Take the picture.

_____ 3. Wind the knob to advance the film.

U. Use the dictionary entry below to answer the questions.

fool (fool) *v.* **1.** to trick: *She fooled me.* **2.** to be silly; tease: *I said I could jump over that building, but I was only fooling.*

n.	noun
pron.	pronoun
v.	verb
adj.	adjective
adv.	adverb
prep.	preposition

1. What part of speech is the word <u>fool</u>? _____

2. Would <u>foot</u> be before or after <u>fool</u>? _____

3. Would <u>firm / fold</u> be the guide words for <u>fool</u>? _____

V. Write <u>title page</u>, <u>copyright page</u>, <u>table of contents</u>, or <u>index</u> to tell where you would find the information.

_____ **1.** the author's name

_____ **2.** the place a book was published

_____ **3.** the page on which specific information can be found

W. Use the sample encyclopedia entry to answer the questions.

CARSON, CHRISTOPHER ("KIT") (1809–1868) was an American trapper and frontiersman. He also served as a guide for pioneers heading west.

1. Who is this article about? _____

2. Is there a cross-reference? _____

_____

Below is a list of the sections on *Check What You've Learned* and the pages on which the skills in each section are taught. If you missed any questions, turn to the pages listed, and practice the skills. Then correct the problems you missed on *Check What You've Learned*.

Section	Practice Page	Section	Practice Page	Section	Practice Page
Unit 1		*Unit 3*		*Unit 4*	
A	5–7	H	31, 32	Q	60–64, 66
B	8	I	34, 35	*Unit 5*	
C	9, 11	J	36, 37, 41	R	73
D	10	K	38, 39	S	74–77, 80, 81
		L	40, 42–45	*Unit 6*	
Unit 2		M	46, 47	T	87
E	16–18, 20, 21	N	48–52	U	88–92
F	23, 24	O	53	V	93
G	25, 26	P	54, 55	W	94

Check What You Know (P. 1)

A. 1. S
2. H
3. A
4. H

B. ball

C. 1. C
2. P
3. S
4. C

D. 1. will not
2. he will

E. The words in bold should be circled.

1. E, **days,** are
2. IN, **you,** do mean
3. D, **I,** like
4. IM, **(You),** should take

F. 1. CS
2. CP

G. 1. RO
2. CS

H. Underline: dog, park. Circle: José, Rachel.

Check What You Know (P. 2)

I. car's

J. 1. H
2. L
3. A

K. 1. future
2. past
3. present

L. 1. Did, see
2. drank, broke
3. written, sung
4. ate, began

M. 1. PP
2. SP
3. OP

N. 1. adjective
2. adverb

O. The words in bold should be circled.
An oil spot was **on** the floor **of** the garage.

Check What You Know (P. 3)

P. 1. Teach
2. good
3. set
4. sit
5. may

Q.
487 E. Deer Run
Sacramento, CA 94099
Feb. 27, 2006

Dear Luke,
What's it like living in California? I can't even imagine it. The postcards you sent were fantastic! It will be fun to come and visit. I'm worried about earthquakes, though.
Take care of yourself.
Your friend,
Paul

R. Discuss your answer with your instructor.

S. Discuss your answers with your instructor.

T. 1. 3
  2. 1
  3. 2

Check What You Know (P. 4)

U. 1. noun
  2. after
  3. yes

V. 1. table of contents
  2. title page
  3. copyright page

W. 1. the parrot
  2. parakeet

Unit 1 Vocabulary

Lesson 1, Synonyms (P. 5)

A. Phrase content will vary. Suggested synonyms:

  1. little, tiny
  2. large, huge
  3. auto, car
  4. choose, pick
  5. end, finish
  6. stream, brook
  7. allow, let
  8. fast, quick

B. Synonyms will vary. Suggested synonyms:

  1. tall
  2. shorter
  3. old
  4. kill
  5. burned
  6. reach

C. Discuss your answers with your instructor.

Lesson 2, Antonyms (P. 6)

A. Antonyms will vary. Suggested antonyms:

  1. light
  2. lazy
  3. down
  4. quiet
  5. south
  6. sell
  7. night
  8. sweet
  9. go
  10. bad
  11. large
  12. smooth
  13. white
  14. below
  15. smiling
  16. over
  17. ugly
  18. hot
  19. weak
  20. narrow
  21. happy
  22. west
  23. warm
  24. start
  25. light
  26. short
  27. take
  28. easy

B. Antonyms will vary. Suggested antonyms:

Line 1.	happy
Line 2.	first
Line 3.	go
Line 4.	exciting, high
Line 5.	cold
Line 6.	first
Line 7.	unpack
Line 8.	outside
Line 9.	wonderful

Lesson 3, Homonyms (P. 7)

A. Phrase content will vary. Suggested homonyms:

1. hall
2. rode
3. some
4. weigh
5. knew
6. meet

B. 1. too, to
   2. two
   3. to, two, too
   4. to, two, to

C. 1. there, their
   2. They're, their
   3. They're, their

Lesson 4, Homographs (P. 8)

A. 1. b
   2. b
   3. a
   4. b
   5. b

B. 1. snap
   2. limp
   3. row
   4. bark
   5. squash

C. Discuss your answers with your instructor.

Lesson 5, Prefixes and Suffixes (P. 9)

A. 1. kindness, the state of being kind
   2. predate, to date before
   3. helpless, without help
   4. remade, made again

B. 1. relives
   2. endless
   3. darkness
   4. predawn
   5. misread
   6. delightful

Lesson 6, Contractions (P. 10)

A. 1. who's
   2. couldn't
   3. they've
   4. I'll
   5. doesn't
   6. should've
   7. you'd
   8. I've
   9. that's
   10. didn't
   11. let's
   12. they're

B. 1. wasn't
   2. Where's
   3. She's
   4. I've
   5. can't
   6. What'll
   7. Let's
   8. he'll
   9. What's
   10. it's
   11. I'm or it's
   12. couldn't

Lesson 7, Compound Words (P. 11)

A. 1. high/way
   2. old/time
   3. full/moon
   4. snow/flake
   5. air/conditioner
   6. fire/drill
   7. bare/foot
   8. baby/sitter
   9. splash/down
   10. sweat/shirt
   11. high/rise
   12. earth/quake
   13. half/mast
   14. bull/dog
   15. skate/board

B. 1. hardware or neighborhood
   2. backyard or neighborhood
   3. afternoon
   4. outcome
   5. neighborhood

C. 1. houseboat, boathouse
2. cupcake, cakewalk

Review (P. 12)

A. 1. A
2. S
3. A
4. H
5. S
6. A
7. S
8. H
9. H
10. S
11. H
12. S
13. H
14. S
15. A

B. 1. pen
2. racket
3. bear
4. clear
5. mean

C. 1. rewire
2. hopeless
3. presoak
4. washable
5. misshapen
6. goodness
7. humorless
8. redo
9. removable
10. preview
11. strangeness
12. misspelled

Review (P. 13)

D. 1. What is
2. They have
3. you will
4. I would
5. they will

E. Sentences will vary. Suggested compound words:
backyard
loudspeaker
nighttime
seashore
toolbox
newspaper

F. The words in bold should be circled.
1. **postcard**, post card
2. **overseas**, over seas
3. **throughout**, through out
4. they're, they are
5. **overdoing**, over doing
6. **everything**, every thing

Using What You've Learned (P. 14)

A. 1. A, S, A, S
2. S, A, A, S
3. S, S, A, S

B. Discuss your answers with your instructor.

C. Discuss your answers with your instructor.

D. Discuss your answers with your instructor.

Using What You've Learned (P. 15)

E. Sentences will vary. Suggested words:
1. useless
2. shyness
3. prepay
4. rewrite
5. miscount
6. readable

F. 1. moonlight
2. frostbite
3. eyeball
4. midnight or midsummer
5. pinpoint

G. Contractions and sentences will vary. Suggested contractions:
1. I'll, you'll, she'll, he'll, it'll, we'll, they'll
2. he's, she's, it's, what's, that's, who's, how's, there's
3. I've, I'll, I'd, I'm

Unit 2 Sentences

Lesson 8, Recognizing Sentences (P. 16)

A. S should precede the following sentences:

3, 6, 7, 9, 10, 12, 13, 15, 17

B. Discuss your answers with your instructor.

Lesson 9, Types of Sentences (P. 17)

A.
1. interrogative
2. declarative
3. interrogative
4. declarative
5. declarative
6. interrogative
7. interrogative
8. declarative

B. Discuss your answers with your instructor.

Lesson 10, More Types of Sentences (P. 18)

A.
1. imperative
2. exclamatory
3. imperative
4. imperative
5. exclamatory
6. imperative
7. exclamatory
8. exclamatory
9. imperative
10. imperative
11. exclamatory
12. imperative
13. imperative
14. exclamatory

B. Discuss your answers with your instructor.

Lesson 11, Complete Subjects and Predicates (P. 19)

A.
1. S   3. P   5. S
2. P   4. S   6. P

B. Discuss your answers with your instructor.

Lesson 12, Simple Subjects (P. 20)

A. The words in bold should be circled.
1. Freshly-picked **morels**/are . . .
2. These **mushrooms**/can . . .
3. A rich **soil**/is . . .
4. Grassy **spots**/are . . .
5. The **spring**/must . . .
6. Damp **earth**/is . . .
7. A clear, sunny **sky**/means . . .
8. **We**/never . . .
9. Tall, wet **grasses**/often . . .
10. **We**/must . . .
11. These spongy little **mushrooms**/do . . .
12. **You**/might . . .

B. Discuss your answers with your instructor.

Lesson 13, Simple Predicates (P. 21)

A. The words in bold should be circled.
1. Many tourists/**visit** the Netherlands in April or May.
2. The beautiful tulip blooms/**reach** their height of glory during these months.
3. Visitors/**can see** flowers for miles and miles.
4. Joan/**is dreaming** of a trip to the Netherlands someday.
5. She/**has seen** colorful pictures of tulips in catalogs.
6. The catalogs/**show** tulips of all colors in full bloom.
7. Joan/**is** anxious to see the tulips herself.
8. Passing travelers/**can buy** large bunches of flowers.
9. Every Dutch city/**has** flowers everywhere.
10. Flower vases/ **can be found** in the cars of some Dutch people.

B. Discuss your answers with your instructor.

C. Discuss your answers with your instructor.

Lesson 14, Understood Subjects (P. 22)

A.
1. (You) Turn
2. (You) Turn
3. (You) Park
4. (You) Do block
5. (You) Leave
6. (You) Help
7. (You) Hold
8. (You) Get
9. (You) Lock
10. (You) Check
11. (You) Knock
12. (You) Try

B. Discuss your answers with your instructor.

Lesson 15, Using Compound Subjects (P. 23)

A.
1. C, Paul Bunyan and Babe
2. Babe
3. C, Maine and Minnesota
4. Babe
5. C, Lumberjacks and storytellers

B.
1. Tennessee and Texas claim Davy Crockett as their hero.
2. Great bravery and unusual skills made Davy Crockett famous.
3. True stories and tall tales about Davy Crockett were passed down.
4. These true stories and tall tales made Davy Crockett a legend.

C. Discuss your answers with your instructor.

Lesson 16, Using Compound Predicates (P. 24)

A.
1. C, wrote and printed its own newspaper.
2. was named editor-in-chief.
3. C, assigned the stories and approved the final copies.
4. were reporters.
5. C, either wrote the news stories or edited the stories.
6. C, interviewed a new student and wrote up the interview.

B. Sentences may vary. Suggested:

1. Jenny covered the baseball game and described the best plays.
2. Sue and Kim wrote jokes and made up puzzles.
3. Luis corrected the news stories and wrote headlines.
4. Alex typed the newspaper but couldn't print it.

C. Discuss your answers with your instructor.

Lesson 17, Simple and Compound Sentences (P. 25)

A.
1. S, George Washington/witnessed
2. C, John Adams/was   his son/was
3. S, Thomas Jefferson/was
4. C, The British/burned President Madison/escaped

B. Sentences may vary. Suggested:

1. Andrew Jackson was called "Old Hickory," and Zachary Taylor's nickname was "Old Rough and Ready."
2. Four presidents had no children, but John Tyler had fourteen children.
3. Chester A. Arthur put the first bathroom in the White House, and Benjamin Harrison put in electric lights.
4. Woodrow Wilson coached college football, and Ronald Reagan announced baseball games on radio.

Lesson 18, Correcting Run-on Sentences (P. 26)

A. 1. marsupials. All
   2. marsupial. The
   3. kangaroos. They . . . kangaroos. Some
   4. Australia. Their

B. Mexico. They
   white. They
   teeth. The
   babies. Each

Review (P. 27)

A. 1. IN
   2. X
   3. D
   4. X
   5. E
   6. IN
   7. IM
   8. X
   9. D
   10. IM
   11. E
   12. D

B. 1. bicycle/was known
   2. wheels/were made
   3. feature/was
   4. (You)/Guess
   5. wheels/came
   6. wheel/increased
   7. wheel/became
   8. They/began using
   9. tire/brought
   10. people/turned

Review (P. 28)

C. 1. SS, SP
   2. CS, SP
   3. SS, CP
   4. CS, CP
   5. SS, CP

D. The words in bold should be circled.
   1. Rain and sleet **are** two forms that water can take.
   2. **Water** also **becomes** snow and hail.
   3. **Wind** tosses and swirls snowflakes into drifts.
   4. **Sunshine** heats and evaporates water.

E. 1. simple
   2. compound
   3. compound
   4. compound
   5. compound

F. Paragraphs will vary. Suggested:

   It was hot in the car, so we rolled down the windows. The air was fresh, and it felt cool on our faces. Larry began to sing. He sang off-key. The song was funny and was one we all knew. Soon we were all singing. We sounded terrible, but we had fun anyway.

Using What You've Learned (P. 29)

A. 1. Discuss your answers with your instructor.
   2. S
   3. S
   4. Discuss your answers with your instructor.
   5. Discuss your answers with your instructor.

B. Discuss your answers with your instructor.

C. Discuss your answers with your instructor.
   1. tornado
   2. storm
   3. had flooded
   4. Homeowners
   5. created
   6. rescued

D. Discuss your answers with your instructor.

Using What You've Learned (P. 30)

E. Discuss your answers with your instructor.

1. opened
2. were given
3. presented
4. received

F. Discuss your answers with your instructor.

1. robber
2. detective
3. bystander
4. clerk

G. Sentences will vary. Suggested:

1. Alex and Steve were writing a play. They wrote together often.
2. This time they couldn't agree, and they argued for hours.
3. Alex would say one thing, and Steve would say the opposite.
4. They were both right, and they were both wrong, but neither would give in.
5. Finally, Alex stood up and said he was leaving.
6. Steve couldn't believe that their argument had caused such a serious problem.
7. They glared at each other, and they started laughing.
8. They decided to forget the problem and work together as a team.

Unit 3 — Grammar and Usage

Lesson 19, Nouns (P. 31)

A. Discuss your answers with your instructor.

B.
1. section, United States, scenes, beauty
2. trees, California, giants, forest
3. fall, tourists, trees, Vermont
4. cities, beaches
5. flowers, grasses, prairies, Texas
6. Montana, Wyoming, mountains
7. citizens, state, pride, charm, state

Lesson 20, Common and Proper Nouns (P. 32)

A. Discuss your answers with your instructor.

B. Common nouns will vary. Suggested:

1. state
2. month
3. holiday
4. woman, girl
5. month
6. state
7. book
8. day
9. province, lake
10. continent
11. man, woman, person, doctor
12. mountains
13. president, man
14. desert
15. city
16. country
17. planet
18. man, boy

Lesson 21, Singular and Plural Nouns (P. 33)

A.
1. P, boot
2. S, armies
3. S, matches
4. P, map
5. P, inch
6. S, feet
7. S, heroes
8. S, alleys
9. S, babies
10. P, woman
11. P, half
12. P, sky
13. S, wives
14. P, box
15. S, beaches
16. S, books

B.
1. stories
2. watches
3. players
4. shelves
5. monkeys
6. children

Lesson 22, Singular Possessive Nouns (P. 34)

A.
1. dog's
2. neighbor's
3. plane's
4. Ann's
5. grandmother's
6. tiger's
7. sister's
8. brother's
9. mother's
10. school's
11. teacher's
12. cat's
13. dinosaur's
14. team's

B.
1. Amanda's friend
2. the friend's car
3. the zoo's keeper
4. the lion's roar
5. the tiger's cage

Lesson 23, Plural Possessive Nouns (P. 35)

A.
1. horses, horse's, horses'
2. birds, bird's, birds'
3. teachers, teacher's, teachers'
4. children, child's, children's
5. trucks, truck's, trucks'
6. doctors, doctor's, doctors'
7. men, man's, men's
8. churches, church's, churches'

B.
1. The Smiths' cat has three kittens.
2. The kittens' names are Frisky, Midnight, and Puff.
3. The neighbors' dogs are very playful.
4. The dogs' pen is in the yard.
5. The cats' curiosity might get them into trouble.

Lesson 24, Action Verbs (P. 36)

A.
1. started
2. recycle
3. buy
4. recycled
5. threw
6. burned
7. harmed
8. asked
9. recycle
10. throw
11. work
12. recycle

B.
1. worried
2. studied
3. hoped, knew, felt, thought
4. thought
5. remember
6. felt
7. hoped, knew, thought, felt
8. believe

Lesson 25, Helping Verbs (P. 37)

A. The words in bold should be circled.
1. **Have** heard
2. **was** born
3. **could** make
4. **were** telling
5. was (no helping verb)
6. **had** climbed
7. **was** carrying
8. **had been** pouring
9. **was** covered
10. **were** running
11. **could** make
12. saw (no helping verb)
13. jumped (no helping verb)
14. did (no helping verb)
15. sing (no helping verb)

B.
1. would
2. have
3. will

Lesson 26, Present and Past Tense (P. 38)

A.
1. tells
2. plays
3. makes
4. call
5. is
6. frightens
7. hits
8. love

B.
1. had reached
2. trailed
3. were called
4. left, went
5. made
6. came
7. went

C. Discuss your answers with your instructor.

Lesson 27, Future Tense (P. 39)

A. Verbs will vary. Suggested:

1. will write, will send
2. will decide
3. will fill
4. will make
5. will bake
6. will think
7. will hide
8. will shout

B.
1. will send
2. will receive
3. will mail
4. will study
5. will choose
6. will plan
7. will write
8. will design
9. will make
10. will hope

Lesson 28, Subject-Verb Agreement (P. 40)

1. P/ stories, tell
2. S/ story, says
3. S/ Wild Dog, becomes
4. P/ dogs, leave
5. S/ dog, doesn't
6. P/ people, don't
7. P/ Diggings, prove
8. P/ Bones, do
9. P/ vases, picture
10. S/ organization, trains
11. P/ eyes, have
12. S/ dog, does
13. S/ person, doesn't

Lesson 29, Agreement with Linking Verbs (P. 41)

A.
1. S/ Tracy, is
2. P/ brothers, are
3. P/ Tracy and her brothers, were
4. S/ Tracy, was
5. P/ brothers, were
6. P/ people, were
7. S/ Tracy, was
8. P/ brothers, were
9. S or P/ you, were
10. S/ Tracy, is

B.
1. is
2. Isn't
3. is
4. was
5. was
6. were
7. are
8. was

Lesson 30, Forms of *Go, Do, See,* and *Sing* (P. 42)

A.
1. did
2. gone
3. sang
4. sung, did
5. seen
6. sung
7. sang
8. went
9. done
10. saw
11. seen
12. did
13. gone
14. sung
15. gone
16. went
17. saw

B. 1. gone
2. done
3. seen
4. sang

Lesson 31, *Break, Drink, Take,* and *Write* (P. 43)

A. 1. took
2. taken
3. wrote
4. drank
5. taken
6. broke
7. wrote
8. written
9. drunk
10. taken

B. 1. taken
2. drunk
3. broken
4. broken
5. written

Lesson 32, *Eat, Draw, Give,* and *Ring* (P. 44)

A. 1. gave
2. eaten
3. ate
4. given
5. eaten
6. gave
7. rang
8. drawn
9. drew
10. rung
11. eaten

B. 1. rung
2. eaten
3. given

Lesson 33, *Begin, Fall, Steal,* and *Throw* (P. 45)

A. 1. begun   8. stolen
2. thrown   9. begun
3. began   10. fell
4. fallen   11. threw
5. threw   12. thrown
6. fell   13. thrown
7. fallen

B. 1. stolen
2. begun
3. thrown
4. begun

Lesson 34, Subject and Object Pronouns (P. 46)

A. 1. She
2. He
3. They
4. She
5. It
6. She
7. she
8. She

B. 1. me
2. us
3. him
4. them
5. us
6. them

Lesson 35, Possessive Pronouns (P. 47)

A. 1. her
2. hers
3. our
4. hers, mine
5. our
6. ours
7. my, hers
8. yours
9. Your
10. Its

B. 1. Its
  2. his
  3. his

Lesson 36, Adjectives (P. 48)

A.

	Adjective	Noun
1.	early, healthy, important	Greeks, body
2.	strong, healthy	bodies, minds
3.	distant	past
4.	great, powerful	god, Cronus
5.	high, beautiful	peaks, mountains
6.	mighty, first, peaceful	struggle, Olympics, valley

B. Discuss your answers with your instructor.

C. Discuss your answers with your instructor.

Lesson 37, Adjectives That Compare (P. 49)

1. biggest
2. largest
3. more interesting
4. larger
5. more accurate
6. higher
7. biggest
8. most popular
9. prettiest
10. greatest
11. finest
12. hardest

Lesson 38, Adverbs (P. 50)

A.

	Verb	Adverb	Tells
1.	had talked	daily	how often
2.	walked	often	how often
3.	had	seldom	how often
4.	decided	suddenly	when
5.	slipped	quietly	how
6.	crept	carefully	how
7.	opened	quietly	how
8.	peered	then	when
9.	swept	instantly	when
10.	banged	loudly	how
11.	ran	swiftly	how
12.	returned	never	how often

B. 1. late
  2. nervously
  3. Suddenly
  4. finally

Lesson 39, Adverbs That Compare (P. 51)

1. closer
2. earlier
3. faster
4. more quickly
5. more patiently
6. more carefully
7. more quietly
8. sooner
9. most skillfully
10. more happily

Lesson 40, Adjectives or Adverbs (P. 52)

	Adjectives	Adverbs
1.	Three, rugged	once
2.	wild	finally, there
3.	different	usually
4.	zoo, three, bear	
5.	young, comfortable, new, distant	soon
6.	hilly, hopeful, six	quietly, then, down
7.	next, rocky, powerful	carefully
8.	huge, brown, three	playfully
9.	two, that	quietly
10.	large	barely
11.	wise	never, uphill
12.	human, watchful, mother	immediately
13.	fierce, beady	heavily, out, up
14.	red, dirty	tightly
15.	curious	clumsily
16.	wide	Quickly, below
17.	wise	successfully

Lesson 41, Prepositions (P. 53)

A. The words in bold should be circled.

1. **on** the dining room table
2. **of** Marta's
3. **for** weeks
4. **in** her bedroom
5. **into** the dining room
6. **to** the floor
7. **to** the dining room
8. **under** the table
9. **on** her face

B. When I went into the store, I looked at coats. I needed a new one to wear during the winter. I left my old one on the bus. When I got off the bus, I noticed it was very hot. I took off my coat and put it under my seat. When I got off the bus, I forgot it. When I asked about it, I was told to look at the office. It was not there.

C. Discuss your answers with your instructor.

Lesson 42, Using *May/Can* and *Good/Well* (P. 54)

1. May
2. may, can
3. well
4. good
5. May
6. can
7. well
8. good
9. may
10. may
11. can
12. can
13. can, well
14. good
15. well
16. good
17. well
18. good
19. can

Lesson 43, Using *Teach/Learn* and *Set/Sit* (P. 55)

1. teach
2. learn
3. teach
4. teach
5. learn
6. sit
7. set, sit
8. sit
9. teach
10. teach
11. sit
12. sit
13. teach
14. learn, set
15. Sit
16. set
17. sit
18. teach, set
19. set

Review (P. 56)

A. Nouns: Kathy, notebook, Thursday
Pronouns: She, it, him, He
Verbs: found, gave, was
Adjectives: Ray's, black, science, thankful

B. The words in bold should be circled.

1. study, will study
2. **learned**, will learn
3. tell, will tell; **plowed**, will plow
4. **grew**, will grow
5. **raised**, will raise

C. 1. sung
2. seen
3. gone
4. did
5. saw
6. sang

Review (P. 57)

D.
1. eaten
2. broke
3. fell
4. begun
5. thrown
6. gave
7. stolen
8. wrote
9. taken
10. drank

E. The words in bold should be circled.
1. at Rosa's house, **shortly**
2. around the house, **closely**
3. by it, **excitedly, too**
4. in her house, **quietly**
5. by their words, **more**
6. at the officers, of the crime, **happily**

F.
1. set
2. learn
3. can
4. good
5. teach
6. learn, well, sit, teach

Using What You've Learned (P. 58)

A.
1. doesn't
2. can
3. their
4. member's
5. her
6. wanted
7. hers
8. I
9. sadder
10. taught, good
11. well
12. learn
13. goes
14. taken
15. larger

B. Line 2. Kentucky's
Line 3. longest
Line 4. has
Line 5. rainiest
Line 6. is, largest
Line 9. He
Line 10. prettiest

Using What You've Learned (P. 59)

C. The words in bold should be circled.

The circus is an exciting show to see. It has been called "The Greatest Show on Earth." Smiling children walk **happily** with their parents into the huge tent. They find seats **quickly** because the brass band is starting to play. The colorful parade will begin in three minutes. **First** comes the ringmaster in his bright red coat and tall hat, parading **importantly** to the center ring.

D. Discuss your answers with your instructor.

E.
1. play's
2. actors'
3. children's
4. parent's
5. audience's

F.
1. hardest
2. brighter
3. more

 Unit 4 Capitalization and Punctuation

Lesson 44, Capitalizing First Words (P. 60)

A. The first letter of each of the following should be circled and capitalized.
1. Have
2. John; Yes
3. So
4. He
5. I
6. We're

B. The first letter of each of the following should be circled and capitalized.

1. There, Lived, And, She
2. If, And, What, And
3. The, Song, Hiawatha
4. Down, River
5. Up, Up, Away
6. A Balloon Ride

Lesson 45, Proper Nouns and Adjectives (P. 61)

A. The first letter of each of the following should be circled and capitalized.

1. Larry
2. Chipper
3. Japanese, Tokyo, Japan
4. Scottish, Scotland
5. Larry, London
6. Sherlock Holmes
7. African, Mali, West Africa
8. Larry, Italian
9. Chipper's, Thailand

B. Discuss your answers with your instructor.

Lesson 46, Titles and Abbreviations (P. 62)

A. The first letter of each of the following should be circled and capitalized.

1. Governor Potter, Senator Williams
2. Dr. Laura Bedford, Mayor Phillips
3. Rev. Barton, Mr. James Adams, Jr.
4. Prince Charles

B. 1. Gen. David E. Morgan
6656 N. Second Ave.
Evanston, IL 60202
2. Valentine's Day Exhibit
at Oak Grove Library
Mon.–Fri., Feb. 10–14
101 E. Madison St.
3. Sgt. Carlos M. Martinez
17 Watling St.
Shropshire SY7 OLW, England
4. Maxwell School Field Day
Wed., Apr. 30, 1:00
Register Mon.–Tues., Apr. 28–29
Mr. Modica's office

Lesson 47, Using End Punctuation (P. 63)

A. 1. .
2. .
3. ?
4. .
5. .
6. ?
7. ?
8. .
9. .

B. Line 2. did?
Line 3. days.
Line 5. grow.
Line 6. built.
Line 7. room./kitchen?
Line 8. fireplace.
Line 9. heat./cold?
Line 10. logs./sleep?
Line 11. loft.
Line 13. themselves.
Line 14. family./land.
Line 15. times?

Lesson 47, Using End Punctuation (P. 64)

C. 1. .
2. ?
3. .
4. .
5. !
6. .
7. .
8. ?
9. .
10. .
11. !; ?
12. .

D. Line 1. Minnesota?
Line 2. lakes.
Line 3. Lake./was!
Line 5. water./great. or great!
Line 7. dinner.
Line 8. Hackensack.
Line 9. Kensack.
Line 10. edge./horizon.
Line 11. was?
Line 12. sweetheart.
Line 13. her./Minnesota. or Minnesota!

Lesson 48, Using Quotation Marks (P. 65)

A.
1. "We . . . today,"
2. "Let . . . see," . . . "whether . . . is."
3. "Will . . . clues?"
4. "Yes," . . . "and . . . clue."
5. "His . . . pleasant,"
6. "Is . . . Bell?"
7. "Mr. . . . telephone," . . . "but . . . mind."
8. "This . . . talks,"
9. "It . . . phonograph,"
10. "You . . . right,"

B.
1. . . . asked, "Where . . . Michelle?"
2. "We . . . ranch,"
3. . . . asked, "Won't . . . cold?"
4. "Yes," . . . Michelle, "but . . . house."
5. "It's . . . tree,"
6. "Come . . . us,"

Lesson 49, Using Apostrophes (P. 66)

1. home's
2. person's
3. Can't
4. don't, something's
5. You'd, you'll
6. architect's
7. what's
8. you'd
9. everyone's
10. Others'
11. everyone's
12. wouldn't, you're
13. home's, you'll

Lesson 50, Using Commas in Sentences (P. 67)

A.
1. Cedarville, Taylorville, Gardner,
2. bridges, roads,
3. basement,
4. bailing, mopping,
5. blocks,
6. shrubs, flowers,
7. away,
8. lucky,

B.
1. asked,
2. side,
3. joke,
4. asked,
5. asked,
6. beams,

Lesson 50, Using Commas in Sentences (P. 68)

C.
1. Tim,
2. Oh,
3. Marie,
4. Well,
5. Ted,
6. No,
7. Oh,
8. Well,
9. Well,
10. Carlos,
11. Yes,
12. Oh,
13. Well,
14. Carlos,
15. Well,

D. Discuss your answers with your instructor.

Review (P. 69)

A. The first letter of each of the following should be circled and capitalized.

1. Last, Montana, Alberta
2. My, Bob, Rocky Mountains
3. The, Snake River
4. We, American
5. I, Glacier Park
6. Bob, Tales, Old, West
7. Dr. Vicenik, Governor Adams's
8. Mrs. Vicenik, Mr. Morrison
9. Ms. Louis, Dr. Vicenik's
10. We, Walter Vicenik, Winston School, Tues., Apr.

B. 1. . or !   6. ?
2. !   7. !
3. ?   8. . or !
4. .   9. . or !
5. .   10. .

Review (P. 70)

C. 1. "Mark, do you know where George is?" asked Donna.
2. "No, I don't," answered Mark.
3. "He's supposed to meet you, Kiko, and me here," she said.
4. Mark asked, "Why didn't you tell us?"
5. "I did!" Donna exclaimed. "Don't you remember our talk yesterday?"
6. "Oh, now I do," said Mark.
7. Donna said, "I'll bet George didn't remember."
8. "Here's Kiko. At least she remembered, and she's ready to help plan the fund-raiser," said Donna.
9. "Oh, I'm sure George will be here," said Mark.
10. "He's always ready to meet new people, talk, and help others out."

D.
955 S. Rimfire
Clayton, MO 64645
Aug. 25, 2006

Dear José,

I can't wait to see you! It's going to be great visiting Mexico City. I know it's now one of the largest cities in the world. I can't imagine such a huge place.

When I went to see Dr. Fulton for my shots, he said, "Eric, my boy, don't worry about anything. Mexico is a wonderful place to visit. I've been there many times and always enjoyed myself."

I said, "Dr. Fulton, did you ever get lost trying to find your way around?" He said he hadn't, but he also always had a good guide. I'm glad I'll have you there to show me around.

Honestly, José, you've got to know how exciting this is! I want to see everything, do everything, and learn everything I can about your country.

Your friend,
Eric

Using What You've Learned (P. 71)

A. Line 1. Have . . . Eugene Field's . . . "The Duel"?
Line 2. Chinese . . . Dutch
Line 3. poet. They . . . fireplace,
Line 5. table.
Line 6. The . . . said, "Bow-wow-wow."
Line 7. "Mee-ow," . . . cat.
Line 8. Then . . . fight. Bits
Line 9. everywhere.
Line 10. The Chinese . . . cried, "Oh, . . . do?"
Line 11. But . . . night.
Line 12. The . . . cat.
Line 13. Many . . . said, "Burglars . . . them."
Line 14. But . . . Chinese . . . poet, "They
Line 15. up, and that's the truth." or !
Line 16. What . . . was!

B. Line 1. Russian . . . The Coming of the Snow
Line 2. Maid." It . . . Russia
Line 3. cold.
Line 4. Ivan . . . Marie . . . children. They
Line 5. neighbor's . . . snow.
Line 6. One . . . Marie . . . idea.
Line 7. "Ivan, let's . . . child," . . . said. "We
Line 8. own."
Line 9. The . . . alive, . . . Maid.
Line 10. She . . . June. Then
Line 11. cloud.
Line 12. "Don't cry, Marie," said Ivan. "Snow . . .
Line 13. sky, . . . September."

Using What You've Learned (P. 72)

C. Line 1. General Dwight David Eisenhower
Line 2. . . . President Eisenhower. In
Line 3. Eisenhower boys. He . . . brothers, Arthur, Edgar, Earl,
Line 4. Roy, and Milton, . . . Abilene, Kansas.
Line 5. morning, noon, and night.
Line 6. brothers' . . . brother's
Line 7. buggy. Dwight, or Ike,
Line 9. feet.
Line 10. His . . . said, "Ike . . . hoeing. He
Line 11. beans, peas, potatoes, corn, cabbage, carrots,
Line 12. beets." "The . . . Lincoln School," she said, "and
Line 13. schoolyard." She . . . Ike's
Line 14. plate.
Line 15. All . . . read. Ike . . . Greek
Line 16. Roman . . . leaders. His
Line 18. Yale University.

D. Discuss your answers with your instructor.

 Unit 5 Composition

Lesson 51, Writing Sentences (P. 73)

A. Discuss your answers with your instructor.

B. Discuss your answers with your instructor.

Lesson 52, Writing Topic Sentences (P. 74)

A. Discuss your answers with your instructor.

B. Discuss your answers with your instructor.

Lesson 53, Writing Supporting Details (P. 75)

A. Sentences 2, 3, 4, and 6 should be underlined.

B. facts

C. Discuss your answers with your instructor.

D. Discuss your answers with your instructor.

Lesson 54, Comparing and Contrasting (P. 76)

A. 1. b
2. b

B. Discuss your answers with your instructor.

Lesson 55, Using Location (P. 77)

A. Line 1. Below me/the ball field/Across
Line 2. the street from the ball field
Line 3. along the street
Line 6. on the ball field
Line 7. away from the street

B. Discuss your answers with your instructor.

C. Discuss your answers with your instructor.

Lesson 56, Topic and Audience (P. 78)

A. Discuss your answers with your instructor.

B. Discuss your answers with your instructor.

C. Discuss your answers with your instructor.

Lesson 57, Clustering (P. 79)

A. Discuss your answers with your instructor.

B. Discuss your answers with your instructor.

Lesson 58, A Descriptive Paragraph (P. 80)

A. 1. patient, kind, generous

B. 1. Possible details follow:

The store is a block away.
The owners' names are Mr. and Mrs. Aggens.
Mrs. Aggens gives large scoops of ice cream.
She doesn't hurry the writer.
The writer had a decision to make.
The store smelled of coffee.
2. The paragraph lacks color and interest.

C. Discuss your answers with your instructor.

Lesson 59, Writing a Descriptive Paragraph (P. 81)

A. 1. house: weathered, old, had never known a paintbrush, whitened; gate: rickety, crooked, hung on only its top hinge
2. breeze: gentle; grass: tall; moved: rippled; peas: sugary; looked: lovely, white, pastel pink, and lavender

B. Discuss your answers with your instructor.

Lesson 60, Revising and Proofreading (P. 82)

During the history of Earth, there have been several ice ages. These were times when giant sheets of ice spread across many parts of Earth. People think that almost one third of the land was covered by these huge sheets of ice.

The last ice age froze so much ocean water that the level of the oceans dropped. Then lots of land appeared that usually lay underwater. When the temperature began to warm up, the ice sheets melted. The ocean levels rose again.

Review (P. 83)

A. Discuss your answers with your instructor.

B. Discuss your answers with your instructor.

C. Sentences 2, 3, and 5 should be underlined.

D. Discuss your answers with your instructor.

Review (P. 84)

E. 1. an emerald
2. shining, turquoise
3. thundering
4. drifted gently
5. bright pink and red
6. bouncy
7. pounding
8. sudden spray

F. Soils come in two basic types. They are clay or sandy. Heavy soil, or clay, has small particles that don't allow much air in. Sandy soil is made of bigger pieces, and this type of soil provides lots of air for plant roots. You should carefully study the type of soil you have before you plant anything.

Using What You've Learned (P. 85)

A. Discuss your answers with your instructor.

B. Discuss your answers with your instructor.

C. Discuss your answers with your instructor.

Using What You've Learned (P. 86)

D. Discuss your answers with your instructor.

E. Discuss your answers with your instructor.

F. Suggested proofreading and revision:

¶try to imagine what the world would be like if there were no People in it. There would be no cities‸towns‸or villages.There would be no bildings of any knind. nobody would be be there to do or make Anything.

Try to imagine what the world would be like if there were no people in it. There would be no cities, towns, or villages. There would be no buildings of any kind. Nobody would be there to do or make anything.

 Unit 6 Study Skills

Lesson 61, Following Directions (P. 87)

1. Peanut Butter Balls
2. cookie sheet, bowl, measuring cup, teaspoon, stirring spoon
3. 1/2 cup
4. wheat germ and sunflower seeds
5. 350°
6. 15 minutes
7. every 5 minutes
8. one teaspoonful
9. 3 hours
10. sesame seeds

Lesson 62, Alphabetical Order (P. 88)

A. 1. m, o
   2. t, u, v

B. 1. 3, 4, 2, 1
   2. 3, 4, 1, 2
   3. 3, 4, 1, 2
   4. 2, 1, 3, 4

C. 1. 2   2. 3   3. 1
   1. 3   2. 1   3. 2

D. Caskey, Louis J.
   Caskey, T.C.
   Lyndale, Paul
   Lyons, Cindy

Lesson 63, Dictionary: Guide Words (P. 89)

A. 1. *Blink, blame, blossom, blast, blaze,* and *blouse* should be checked.
   2. *Into, introduce, iron, inward, invent, irrigate,* and *invite* should be checked.

B. 1. meanwhile, melody, mention
   2. professor, program, propeller, protest
   3. receive, recess, reckon, recognize
   4. miss, mist, mite

Lesson 64, Dictionary: Syllables (P. 90)

1. chem-i-cal
2. gas-o-line
3. de-gree
4. mar-vel-ous
5. dis-ap-pear
6. chim-ney
7. con-ti-nent
8. mis-er-a-ble
9. gen-er-al-ly
10. gla-cier
11. a-rith-me-tic
12. ex-er-cise
13. hos-pi-tal
14. prob-lem
15. win-dow
16. lan-guage
17. ag-ri-cul-ture
18. par-a-keet
19. be-gin-ning
20. sim-ple
21. de-ter-mine
22. mu-si-cian
23. sal-a-ry
24. chee-tah
25. in-ter-rupt
26. den-tist
27. re-cog-nize
28. ras-cal
29. in-no-cent
30. ed-u-cate
31. a-chieve-ment
32. dar-ling
33. home-stead
34. cal-en-dar
35. mis-sion-ar-y
36. fare-well
37. a-lu-mi-num
38. bac-te-ri-a
39. pro-gram
40. ba-nan-a

Lesson 65, Dictionary: Pronunciation (P. 91)

A. 1. fork or song
   2. about, taken, pencil, lemon, or circus
   3. at
   4. it

B. 1. abandon   10. weight
   2. backstroke   11. wail
   3. clench   12. vision
   4. dainty   13. freight
   5. height   14. hour
   6. entirely   15. diamond
   7. wither   16. satellite
   8. noise   17. migrate
   9. ought   18. angle

Lesson 66, Dictionary: Definitions (P. 92)

A. 1. 4; 2; 1
   2. noun
   3. adjective
   4. audience, auditorium

B. 1. 1
   2. 3
   3. 2

Lesson 67, Parts of a Book (P. 93)

A. 1. index
   2. title page
   3. title page
   4. copyright page
   5. table of contents
   6. copyright page

B. 1. Language Exercises
   2. 73
   3. 82, 84, 86, 109
   4. 2006
   5. none listed
   6. 74
   7. inside back cover
   8. 16
   9. 2, 53, 105, 113
   10. Forms of *Break, Drink, Take,* and *Write*

Lesson 68, Using an Encyclopedia (P. 94)

A. 1. water
    2. a person can live only a few days without water; water is necessary for all living things
    3. about 60 percent
    4. by eating and drinking
    5. oxygen
    6. air; liquid
    7. Living things need both to live.
    8. no
    9. A gas that has no smell, no taste, and no color.
    10. air

Lesson 68, Using an Encyclopedia (P. 95)

B. 1. Anthony
    2. salt
    3. New
    4. Scotland
    5. Rio
    6. United
    7. literature
    8. horses

C. 1. 3
    2. 20
    3. 8
    4. 20
    5. 17
    6. 10
    7. 17
    8. 19

Review (P. 96)

A. 1. to Peter's house
    2. 2
    3. Creekway
    4. north
    5. a stop sign

B. 1. traffic, transatlantic
    2. trample; trăm′ pəl
    3. traffic, trance
    4. transatlantic
    5. trance
    6. tranquil, transatlantic
    7. trample
    8. calm; peaceful; free from disturbance

Review (P. 97)

C. 1. locks
    2. help ships move through canals
    3. two
    4. stairs
    5. canal

D. The words in bold should be circled.
    1. 5, **mining**
    2. 7, **Twain**
    3. 5, **Nile**
    4. 7, **tundra**
    5. 7, **Sweden**
    6. 3, **Great**
    7. 3, **gardens**
    8. 8, **volcanoes**

E. 1. title page
    2. index
    3. copyright page
    4. table of contents
    5. copyright page

Using What You've Learned (P. 98)

A. 1. enough to taste
    2. 1 cup

B. 1. academy
    2. accompany

C. 1. slum-ber
    2. smat-ter-ing
    3. slug-gish

D. 1. table of contents
    2. copyright page
    3. index
    4. title page

Using What You've Learned (P. 99)

E. Discuss your answers with your instructor.

F. The words in bold should be circled.

  1. **Springfield**, 18, 10
  2. **vegetables**, 20, 11
  3. **Great**, 8, 5
  4. **boxcars**, 2, 3
  5. **snowshoe**, 18, 9
  6. **bee**, 2, 2
  7. **zipper**, 21, 12
  8. **monkey**, 13, 7
  9. **Disney**, 5, 4
  10. **melons**, 13, 6
  11. **aspirin**, 1, 1
  12. **Paraguay**, 16, 8

 Final Reviews

Final Review, Unit 1, (P. 100)

1. A	6. A	11. S
2. S	7. H	12. A
3. H	8. S	13. H
4. A	9. H	14. S
5. S	10. A	15. A

1. mum	4. pupil
2. punch	5. stir
3. can	6. tip

1. unhappy	5. preview
2. reread	6. endless
3. misunderstood	7. dependable
4. repairable	8. helpful

Final Review, Unit 1 (P. 101)

1. Let us
2. We have
3. I am
4. They have
5. cannot
6. Could not

1. waterfall
2. playmate
3. understand
4. powerplant

The words in bold should be circled.

1. **firefighter**, fire, fighter
2. **roadway**, road, way
3. wasn't, was not
4. **treetop**, tree, top
6. couldn't, could, not

Final Review, Unit 2 (P. 102)

Numbers 2 and 4 are sentences.

  1. IN
  2. E
  3. IM
  4. D
  5. IN
  6. E

  1. industry/makes
  2. bee/can fly
  3. honeybee/makes
  4. lifetime/is
  5. bees/make
  6. material/is
  7. material/is
  8. Bees/cannot defend
  9. fly/can kill
  10. Robber flies/kill

Final Review, Unit 2 (P. 103)

1. Planets and moons/revolve around, other bodies in space.
2. Mercury and Venus/revolve around the sun in less than a year.
3. The nine planets in our solar system/rotate and spin like tops.

Sentences 1, 3, 4, and 7 are compound sentences.

Sentences will vary. Suggested:

1. Laura tried to fix her car. She changed the oil, and she put in a new air filter.
2. It worked. It ran well. She had done a good job.

Paragraphs will vary. Suggested:

Sometimes we hop in the car when we get restless. We just drive wherever we choose. It's fun and relaxing. We laugh and forget about our problems. After a while, we have gone far enough. We turn around and drive back home.

Final Review, Unit 3 (P. 104)

1. actors, actor's, actors'
2. babies, baby's, babies'
3. beaches, beach's, beaches'
4. horses, horse's, horses'
5. women, woman's, women's
6. children, child's, children's

The following words should be underlined.

1. was	3. is	5. gaze
2. got	4. will guard	

The following words should be circled.

1. are	4. threw	7. chose
2. went	5. began	8. take
3. sounded	6. drew	9. was

Final Review, Unit 3 (P. 105)

1. P, your
2. S, I
3. S, They
4. O, me
5. S, He
6. S, I

The words in bold should be circled.

After several hours, Jake began to talk **quietly.** He wondered what the most beautiful place in Texas was. Susan said that Austin was prettier than any other city. Tom **loudly** disagreed. He spoke **knowingly** of the golden sands and blue waters of Galveston. Susan **gently** reminded him that it had been a long time since he had been **there**. His wonderful memories might **not** be entirely accurate.

The words in bold should be circled.

1. Before we reached Austin, it grew hot **inside** the car.
2. As we traveled **down** the highway, we began to see changes.
3. The flat land became more hilly as we got closer **to** Austin.
4. We looked **for** signs **of** cowboys and ranches.
5. Our idea **of** Texas was influenced **by** the movies we had seen.

1. can
2. learning
3. sit
4. good
5. teaching
6. well

Final Review, Unit 4 (P. 106)

The letters in bold should be circled.

1. **i** have always wanted to visit **y**ellowstone **n**ational **p**ark.
2. **j**eri and **i** decided to go see it in **m**arch, before the crowds arrived.
3. **w**e almost stayed in **w**yoming because the **g**rand **t**eton **m**ountains were so beautiful.
4. **c**ody was a wonderful town, founded by **c**olonel **w**illiam **f. c**ody, better known as **b**uffalo **b**ill.
5. **h**owever, the book we were reading, *the history of the old west* by **d**r. **e. j. j**ames, convinced us to go on to **c**alifornia.
6. **w**e stopped in **l**as **v**egas, **n**evada, to send postcards back to our friends in **m**issouri.
7. **a**ll **j**eri could talk about was seeing **o**ld **f**aithful, the most famous geyser in the world.
8. **i** bought a book of black-and-white photographs by **a**nsel **a**dams that was magnificent.

1. 1872.
2. park,; there.
3. Moose, deer, antelope, bear,; park.
4. there!
5. canyons, waterfalls, lakes, forests,; meadows.
6. park.
7. sky?
8. feet,; feet.
9. is!
10. Yes,; treasure.

Final Review, Unit 4 (P. 107)

1. "Have you seen Pat's new car?" asked. James.
2. "No, I haven't yet," said Diane.
3. "What kind did he get?" she asked.
4. "I don't know for sure," said James, "but I know it's red."
5. Diane said, "How do you know that?"
6. "He always said that's what he'd buy," said James.
7. "He could've changed his mind," said Diane.
8. James said, "Not Pat. He's not the kind of person who'd do that."
9. "Well," said Diane, "let's go see it now."
10. "Let's go!" said James.
11. "Wow!" said Diane. "That's a great car!"
12. "Pat, where did you get it?" asked James.
13. "I got it at the car lot downtown," said Pat.

1309 W. Harriman St.
Maysville, KY 40419
Sept. 17, 2006

Dear Shelley,

You won't believe what happened! We went to a melodrama, a kind of play, and I became an actor. Yes, it's true. Can fame and fortune be far behind? Here's what happened. We were just sitting there, ready to boo the villain, when the stage manager came out and asked, "Is there a volunteer in the audience?" Before I knew what was happening, Deanna had grabbed my elbow and pushed my hand into the air. The stage manager pointed at me and said, "Come on up here and tell us all your story."

Well, I nearly fainted, of course, but I had no choice. So, I did it, and it was the most fun I've had in a long time. I acted out the part of a woman who refuses a hero's help. He tried to save me from paying rent to a horrible landlord, but I took care of him myself. Then the hero shook my hand and rode off into the sunset. It was so funny! Deanna has pictures, and I can't wait to show them to you.

See you soon,
Ellen

Final Review, Unit 5 (P. 108)

Discuss your answers with your instructor.

Discuss your answers with your instructor.

Sentences 1, 3, and 4 should be underlined.

1. b   2. a   3. b

Final Review, Unit 5 (P. 109)

Discuss your answers with your instructor.

Discuss your answers with your instructor.

Lakes are bodies of water with land all around. They do not connect to the ocean. Most lakes contain fresh water, although a few have salt water. Some very large lakes are called seas.

Final Review, Unit 6 (P. 110)

1. 2   2. 1   3. 4   4. 3

Poems 3; 1, 2
Stories of Real People 4; 1, 2
Fiction 2; 2, 1
Articles 1; 2, 1

The following words should have a check (✓) before them.

1. eggplant, eight
2. harm, hare, harp

The following words should be underlined.

1. cinder
2. nation
3. harp

Final Review, Unit 6 (P. 111)

1. table of contents
2. index
3. title page
4. copyright page

A.
1. bran
2. the outer layers of food grains
3. when making flour
4. dark brown
5. wheat
6. fiber, cereal

B. The words in bold should be circled.

1. **swim**, 7
2. **San**, 7
3. **dentistry**, 2
4. **ant**, 1
5. **Tubman**, 8
6. **syrup**, 7
7. **yawn**, 9
8. **cats**, 1

Check What You've Learned (P. 112)

A. 1. H   2. A   3. S   4. A

B. saw

C. 1. P   2. S   3. C   4. C

D. 1. do not   2. I will

E. The words in bold should be circled.

1. IN, **you**, are going
2. D, **I**, am going
3. E, **You**, can do
4. IM, **You**, do

F. 1. CP   2. CS

G. 1. RO   2. CS

H. *Years, jail,* and *crimes* should be underlined. *Judge Merkle* and *Harold Jones* should be circled.

Check What You've Learned (P. 113)

I. workers'

J. 1. A   2. L   3. H

K. 1. future   2. present   3. past

L. 1. went, took   3. given, threw
   2. drank, began   4. stole, fell

M. 1. PP   2. SP   3. OP

N. 1. adverb   2. adjective

O. The words in bold should be circled.

Under the leaves was a small kitten that had been left **by** its mother.

Check What You've Learned (P. 114)

P. 1. may   3. teach   5. Can
   2. well   4. Sit

908 S. Greenslope
St. Paul, MN 60598
Mar. 11, 2006

Dear Sara,
   I've finally grown to like this job. Who would've dreamed that would happen? Do you remember how much I hated it when I got here?
   Everyone said, "Emily, you'll love it if you give it a chance." Well, they were right!
   You'd like it here, but I know you won't come. Write to me soon.
                              Your sister,
                              Emily

R. Discuss your answers with your instructor.

S. Discuss your answers with your instructor.

T. 1. 1   2. 3   3. 2

Check What You've Learned (P. 115)

U. 1. verb   2. after   3. no

V. 1. title page
   2. copyright page
   3. index

W. 1. Christopher "Kit" Carson   2. no